The Heartless Traffic:
New and
Selected
Poems

For Avril and Stephen,

Most warmly

[signature]

28/9/2021

The Heartless Traffic:
New and Selected Poems

Jeremy Robson

smoke
STACK
BOOKS

Smokestack Books
1 Lake Terrace, Grewelthorpe, Ripon HG4 3BU
e-mail: info@smokestack-books.co.uk
www.smokestack-books.co.uk

Cover image:
David Abse,
Night Driver

Author photo:
KT Bruce

ISBN 9781916139220

Smokestack Books
is represented
by Inpress Ltd

for Carole,
as always

You seem to think I've
been remote all day.
It's true, I have, and can
only say in my defence
that unbidden thoughts
and words were vying to
find some order in my head.

You mustn't mind. I'll soon
emerge, and hopefully there'll
be a pattern on a page that
makes some sense, makes
it all worthwhile, may
even make you smile.

By the same author

Poetry
Poems for Jazz (Leslie Weston Publications, 1963)
Thirty Three Poems (Sidgwick and Jackson, 1964)
Poems Out of Israel (Turret Books, 1970)
In Focus (Allison and Busby, 1970)
Blues in the Park (Smokestack Books, 2014)
Subject Matters (Smokestack Books, 2017)

As Editor
The Young British Poets (Chatto and Windus, 1971)
Corgi Modern Poets in Focus (Vol. 2 and 4, 1971)
Poems from Poetry and Jazz in Concert (Souvenir Press, 1972)
Poetry Dimension 1 (Sphere Books, 1973)

Prose
Under Cover: A Poet's Life in Publishing (Biteback, 2018)

Contents

from *Blues in the Park*

Introduction

It's strange, turning back, re-reading the poems I wrote with passion and pride over fifty years ago. Where is the young man I was? They meant everything to me then, as did my first real book, *Thirty Three Poems,* published by a leading London publisher, the publisher of Rupert Brooke among others. 'I'm a poet', I could declare, if only to myself. Looking back now I wonder at such ill-judged precocity. Yet even so, there are a few poems in that fledgling volume that still speak, if rawly, of a time and place, and at the gentle insistence of my sage publisher they are included here, together with a handful of other early ones, published in magazines but not included in my early books. (I have tried to resist the temptation to tweak them.) At that time I was, after all, that boy, that young man, and I suppose that in one's early years the focus of attention is all too often oneself. The French poets, who I read avidly at that stage in my life, are perhaps more open about this than their English counterparts, with their talk of *l'amour, les larmes,* and *la mort.*

By the time *In Focus* was published I was some six years older and hopefully the poems in that volume are more crafted and draw on experiences that were more, well, experienced. It's been out of print for many years and I'm grateful for the chance to re-introduce some of the poems here, as I was to Allison and Busby for publishing them in the first place.

Then the gap, a very long gap, which I jokingly called the longest writing block in literary history, pointing out that Rimbaud stopped writing at a very young age. But I was not Rimbaud, and well aware of that indisputable fact. What caused it? Well, perhaps my total involvement in the world of publishing, and the strains, financial and emotional, caused by running our own company, and steering it through often stormy waters for more than thirty years. Perhaps not.

When I first thought about going into publishing, a director of Faber, Morley Kennerley, was kind enough, through an introduction, to give me some of his time and tell me a little about the facts of publishing life. Later he wrote me a salutary letter, which I still have, warning: 'Remember that to be a poet in publishing is rather like trying to be a prostitute by day and a virgin by night'. I came to know what he meant, though I have spent a long life trying to be neither of those things! During that fallow period, I found it hard to even talk about poetry, feeling a fraud when I did, though I remained close to a number of the poets who'd become close friends over those early years. 'A poet is only a poet when he is writing a poem', my very dear friend Dannie Abse once wrote, and I understood only too well.

My involvement with *Poetry and Jazz in Concert*, of which there were over 300 large-scale concerts and about which I have written at length elsewhere, gave me the opportunity to read a number of those early poems to mainly young audiences, and to do so alongside a number of established poets from whom I hope I learned. Meeting and teaming up with the pianist/composer Michael Garrick, in many ways a kindred spirit, made these concerts not only possible but a success. The music he wrote was often breathtaking, and the musicians he brought with him were the best in the land. It was a privilege to share a stage with them. It was a rewarding and exciting time, and those many fine poets who became regulars welcomed the opportunity to read to large enthusiastic audiences, some of whom doubtless came for the jazz and found themselves listening to the poems with equal enjoyment, queuing to buy books in the interval. We weren't the Beatles, but that was the era, when ears and eyes were open wide for new experiences, and we even recorded a concert at the Abbey Road studios. People still come up to me in the strangest of places saying that they were at this or that concert or reading, perhaps even at the first Hampstead Town Hall concert, or at one festival or another. It makes me believe it really happened.

I should add that mostly the jazz, original, disciplined and specially written by Michael Garrick, was played *between* the readings, but Michael did set some poems to Jazz, not just my own, but also those of various other participating poets: I have included here a few of the ones he set of mine. Generally, these are rhythmic, lyrical and simple in line, and though written for the page, lent themselves to Garrick's sensitive settings, or so it seemed to me. The exception to all these is 'Blues for the Lonely' written one very blue night many years ago to Miles Davis' *Blue in Green*, as it spun on my portable gramophone in my lonely room.

The later poems from *Blues in the Park* and from *Subject Matters* were written over the past ten years and after the gap I mentioned earlier. I leave them to speak for themselves. They may not be by that young man I spoke of earlier, but I imagine he's in there somewhere.

The same may be true of the new poems that open this volume, which have come, one by one, as a surprise, though they have been hard fought for. Occasionally, looking back, I notice that certain themes return or are echoed, albeit clad in very different garments, even with that wall of time between them. I hadn't realised this, but I suppose that deep down one is always the person that one was, despite all the disguises.

And I suppose too that one is entitled to be one's own influence.

Jeremy Robson,
London 2020

New Poems

The Right Hand

Chance played me the right hand that night.
If I hadn't gone on a last-minute whim
to a party I'd crashed and been let in,
I'd never have met the exotic young girl
who was to bring to my life a landscape
of mosques, camels, deserts and pyramids,
of falafel, pitta bread, mangoes and molokhia,
the songs of Dalida and Charles Trenet,
the beaches and magic of Alexandria
and the great river that splits Cairo in two.

And she, for her part, would never
have met the fallible young man who
was to bring into her life a rather more
restrained landscape of palaces, parks,
monuments and churches, of roast beef,
kippers, porridge and custard, of cream
teas by the Thames, of jazz, poetry and
seaside holidays in the English rain.

It would never have been the same.

The Heartless Traffic

So much drama waiting to be unleashed,
though for the moment, poker-faced, cold,
the large screen waits impassively in the
silence of a curtained room. Yet nothing
will come to be unless I turn the switch
to On, and so decree.

There'll be no ashen-faced political set-tos,
no panicking herds fleeing a lion's claws,
no thrilling shoot-outs at Wembley or the
OK Corral, no arrow piercing Harold's eye...
and poor, tormented, soliloquising
Hamlet will never decide.

With radio too, on/off, on/off, much
the same, an endless power game.

Last night, as I drove abstractedly through
the hypnotic darkness of a motorway,
La Traviata rose towards its heart-breaking climax.
A live performance it might have been,
but there was death in the air.

Overwhelmed by the beauty of the music
and Violetta's impending demise, I pulled into
a lay-by and turned the radio's switch to Off.

While I'm in control, I told myself, she'll never die.
Rain, like tears, was running down the window pane.
Passing cars flashed their lights uncaringly.

If only we could press the pause button
in real life, cry Stop when tragedy looms,
death is about to strike. But when fiction
becomes fact there's no release from that,
no lay-by to pull into, no turning the engine off.

Eventually I switched the radio back on. Just the
sound of applause. The audience, I imagined,
now on its feet, the singers, the conductor, taking
well-earned bows, flowers from the wings.
Freed from the plot, Violetta, hand in hand
with her lover Alfredo, had sprung back to life.
A true diva, she'd live to die another night.

As the applause gave way to an announcer's
voice I turned the key and waited for the
engine to revive. Then, pulling back onto
the motorway, I joined the heartless traffic
in its endless race to God knows where.

So much drama waiting there.

Back in Touch

It was in a way, for me, like coming
back from the dead, or so I surmised, never
myself having made that improbable journey.

Tentative at first, I scribbled the words
that had invaded my head, scrutinising
them hard, then allowing others to follow,
slowly at first and then ever more swiftly,
fearing they might somehow escape.

And then there, finally, it was, laid out
on the page. I'd broken my duck.

Slowly, carefully, I read it forwards and
backwards, backwards and forwards,
not quite believing my luck, changing
the odd word, adding others, removing
what clichéd adjectives I could.

I'd done it, after all those silent years,
and slowly others followed, as if down
a winding narrow path in the dark.
I called it a poem and no one, however
critical, can take it away.

And there it remains today, staring back
at me from the once blank white page,
a landmark only important to me, I know,
which is, I'm sure, how it should be.

Old Norman Ways

It should have been a relaxed postprandial stroll
down a quiet country lane, and so it was until
three small dried-up corpses caught my bleary eyes.
I blinked, thinking that drink had got the better
of me, but no, there they were, folded over the top
of the barbed wire fence skirting a nearby field.
Rats, I thought, but why, gazing like that at the evening
sky through what must once have been their eyes?

Though they'd stopped me dead in my tracks, I wasn't
as dead as they quite clearly were. How long they'd
been hanging there I couldn't say, but from the look
of them it must have been for quite some while.

'Not rats,' the farmer informed us laughingly when
next we met, shrugging his large Gallic shoulders,
'they're moles' – a laughing matter for him perhaps,
steeped in his country ways, but not for us, and
certainly not for the moles he'd trapped and hung there.
'An old Normandy custom,' he said. 'Hang a dead mole
at the boundary of your field, and live ones will keep away.'
'Flee for their lives,' is what I thought he'd say!

I looked at his field, not a molehill in sight, only some
lambs that bleated appealingly as we passed. No
doubt their fate too was in his questionable hands.
Returning silently to our own small garden further
up the lane, nothing but molehills everywhere, a
battle long lost. Hardly a patch of green to be seen.

That night I lay sleepless, thinking of that cruel local
custom. An old Norman one it might have been, but
what else did they protect themselves from I wondered?
Demons, heretics and witches in the superstitious past?
The dukes and barons who had ruled their lands
with iron hands? The Germans who'd invaded them?

From early on it seems we've always needed something
to protect us – flying phalluses carved on the pillars
and gateways of mighty Rome to keep the evil eye at bay,
still worn on amulets today, a scroll on the doorposts of
Jewish homes, the walls of many Middle Eastern houses
painted blue, and blue stones too on rings, bracelets
and necklaces to keep that same feared eye away.

So many old and trusted practices, but when armies invade
and evil reigns, when doors are smashed and families
dragged away, what use are they I asked myself as I turned
uncomfortably under the protective covers of my bed,
nothing but negative thoughts swamping my head?

Next day, passing that field again in the full-on sun, they
were still hanging there, those withered moles, but at the
back of the field I spotted a line of small mounds, the fresh
earth slowly rising. It was as if an underground army was on
the march, and as my mind began to clear I wanted to cheer,
realising that a battle lost can become a battle won, marvelling
as the moles moved their hills forward defiantly, one by one.

All Change

The season's change is all too swift,
and the clothes I moth-balled away
when winter froze are now on call again.
But they seem to have shrunk, be past
their sell-by dates and down a size or two.
There's not much I can do.

Or is it me, swelling round the waist.
I'm breathing in, but can't hold that
for long. I'll have to let them out or
take me in, though however much I
starve or run a daily mile I'll never be that
thin, nor back in style, and nor will they.

I'll have to start again, give these away,
go on a shopping spree and hope I'll find
some new clothes that will do, and that
they, and I, will see the season through.

The Visit

I was prepared for many things,
for memories to arrow through
my head, even for tears, as I edged
cautiously towards their resting place
and the reality of finality confronted me.
But I wasn't prepared for that.

It was a visit long postponed,
but one of silent connection as
I recited to myself the haunting
words of the Kaddish, which speaks
of life, not death, and was their due.

Slowly, bracing myself, I faced anew
those names, once so human, that now
stared back at me from the implacable
white stone, names that remained
a pulsating part of my continuing life.
I took in the dates, and the carefully
crafted words surrounding them.

I was prepared for that, but not
for the large soot-black cat that
caught my eye as I stood in silence,
slinking stealthily towards me, casting
its shadow over the marble slabs so
brilliantly spotlit by the August sun.

What did it mean, this eerie intrusion
into the tranquil scene? Was that cat bringing
luck or something more sinister, which
is how it seemed to me as I moved away,
taking with me something I didn't wish
to take, thoughts of a disturbing kind,
of witches and broomsticks, of cauldrons
and restless spirits, unsettling my mind.
Were there voices in the air?

It remained there staring at me,
commanding the scene, holding its
ground, making me resolve to return
again next day, just to make sure all was
well, just to break any lingering spell.

In the Mood

The songs we shared will always bring
me back to you. Invariably they were sad and rarely
new, about love and loss and years gone by,
songs we'd dance to cheek to cheek on Saturday
nights when lights were low and passion high.

Holding each other tight we hoped the final
bars would never come, that the LPs
spinning on the old Dansette record player
someone would bring, would spin for ever.
Such evenings weren't meant to end.

Even now the poignant melodies queue in my
head like discs in a jukebox, waiting for release.
There are lines of poems that do that too,
touching on moments and memories, and while
their thoughts and rhymes may be more refined,
their sentiments are often similar in kind.

There's no summoning them, those classic
numbers, they arrive unbidden, just as the
indelible scent of the perfume you always
wore still does, suddenly filling a room you
haven't entered, making me catch my breath
as it used to all those years ago.

Nightingales may sing on in Berkeley Square,
and the roses of Picardy will always have their
poignant history, but nothing will replace for me
the beauty of Benny Goodman's *Stardust*,
the Sinatra songs to which we danced, entranced,
or the hypnotic beat of Glenn Miller's *In the Mood*,
played again and again each week.

For we were always in the mood, never
dreaming a day would come when we'd
be summoned by some distant orchestra
to take our places for a final waltz.

And should that dark day come I pray
I may be allowed to sit that last waltz out,
to leave with an altogether more up-beat finale,
something with a spring in it you would have
tapped your feet to, joined in, *Take the A Train*
perhaps, or Bing, or Goodman's swing,
so when I go I'm sure to hear the angels sing.

Coming To

I like to wake up slowly, to silence.
It's always been that way since very young
as I cautiously enter the breaking day.

Whatever the clock might say, night always
seems to linger, the array of people crowding
my head as I breathed in sleep remaining with
me, coming as they did from somewhere deep.

What made me think of him, or her, I wonder,
after years long lost, or seemingly so? Nothing
ever is. Mostly I enjoy their company, and the
unexpected scenes, though some disturb, and
there are those that scare, meaningful at times,
at times bizarre, the real and the surreal interwoven
in a complex web making no sense at all.

As light creeps in and I face familiar walls, I wonder
which world is real, which make-believe. I'm never sure.
Give me time to stare, to think, to be with myself,
come gradually to. Don't let those landscapes sink,
don't disturb, don't pull me from the brink.

Dannie's Park

with thanks to Geoffrey Paul

It seemed as large as a continent,
that magical park I'd hurry to whenever
I stayed with my religious grandparents
in their rambling old house in Leeds.

Still too young to venture there alone,
I'd badger an older relative or friend
to accompany me so I could kick a
ball around, dodging the flower beds
that dotted the extensive lawns, and
bowl at makeshift stumps.

Sepia postcards in my mind recall the
large open-air bathing pool we'd rush to
on timeless summer days, and the wooden
jetty on the lake from where we'd throw
bread to inquisitive swans and stare at
quicksilver fish until the falling sun threw
shadows over the rippling water.

Roundhay Park, the name itself still
retains a hold over me stronger even than
the larger-than-life heroes in the biblical
stories my bearded grandfather would read
to us in front of the large log fire in his draughty
sitting room, while I sat mesmerised by
the glowing embers in the grate and by the
dramatic exploits he'd powerfully relate.

But they couldn't really compete, those awesome
characters and tales, with the exciting park and
the clattering trams we'd catch to get there once
the Sabbath was over and we had the all-clear.

*****

Those adventurous visits ended abruptly
when my father's parents went heaven's way,
to be replaced by Hampstead's extensive heath,
which became, with its ponds and endless
twists and turns, my teenage stomping ground.

I climbed the giant trees in the wooded areas,
bow in hand, thinking I was Robin Hood and
this Sherwood Forest, where he'd rob the rich
to give to the poor – something, despite my
early socialist leanings, I could never quite
bring myself to do as I dreamt the days away.

At Easter and Whitsun there were always several
music-blaring fairs, and I and my friends would
hurry to the ghost train, devouring candy floss,
and commandeer the bumper cars, cutting each
other up, preparing for life. The thrill, and the pungent
smell of fried onions and hamburgers linger still.

Later, when girls came distractingly on the scene,
Sundays by the lake at Regent's Park were the
competing draw, and when luck struck we'd
help this or that one onto a narrow wooden
boat and row her manfully, trying not to splash
or overturn, seeing what favours we could earn.

*****

Wild oats sowed, married and the father of two,
we'd walk our twin daughters in Golders Hill Park,
bordering Hampstead Heath, looking at the deer and
the flamboyant flamingos, at the watchful owls
and exotic birds in the park's mini zoo, delighting
the children, taking their breath away.

These many years on, I continue to walk regularly
in this gem of a park, thinking back, searching
for words, as I pass the spacious animal enclosures
and stroll towards the Victorian grandstand and
the Italian café on the hill, sometimes pausing there
to watch the ducks perform their amusing cabaret.

This was 'Dannie's Park', a mutual friend who lived
nearby declared when I told him of my frequent
wanderings there. And indeed, in many ways it was
and is, for this is where the poet Dannie Abse loved
to stroll, as I do now, lines and poems forming in
his head as he stared abstractedly at the primroses
and daffodils that heralded a new season.

Dannie's Park, especially after the crash that snatched
his wise and gentle wife Joan from him in one of life's
cruel turns, leaving him shaken in mind and body.
I visualise him there, his landmark mane of thick
white hair, whenever I approach the bench by the café,
thinking no doubt of his lost muse, searching for
a word, *the* word, for there are many words, he
always said, but for a poem only one right one.

And nearby, stretched out on the ground, leaning
backwards on her arms, in pale blue shorts and
a singlet through which her breasts protrude,
sandals lying casually beside her long bare legs,
the elegant statue of a girl waits invitingly.

There should be a plaque there for Dannie,
with a line or two from one of his poems.
It would be his Poet's Corner where friends and
admirers could gather once a year, read a few
poems, chat and laugh as he'd always do,
keeping his name alive as we endeavour to.

And hopefully that long-limbed girl he would not
have failed to notice, would still be there, listening
invitingly, ready to chat. He'd have welcomed that.

*****

The seasons turn and the years burn, in
Golders Hill, in Roundhay Park, as in the many
other parks we've visited over the years, but
spring and summer always return, and so I take
my turn, stepping up, filling the pages as best
I can, while the impassive lady in blue looks on,
her smile and falling hair firmly in place, waiting,
watching to see who next will take the stage,
as the sun revives or the lengthy winters rage.

The Nights I Fear

These are the nights I fear, nights
when sleep repels, when words spin
like plates on bamboo sticks,
round and round hypnotically.

Eventually, as thoughts, not
always comfortable, overwhelm me,
I'll stumble out of bed to scribble
in the dark, compulsively.

To turn on lights would break the spell.
This is a private tryst between me and
me, to be engaged in stealthily.

Even then, sleep comes fitfully,
and as soon as day intrudes I'm there
again, staring at scattered pages
I thought I'd left my mark on, at a
trail of letters, words, hieroglyphics
of which I make neither head nor tail.

Perhaps that's how life is, neither
heads nor tails, and I should leave it thus,
not persist, not try to make some order
out of chaos, when none, it seems, exists.

False Alarm

They are numbers I chose myself,
easy to remember, breaking the rules,
but I still hesitate on the doorstep while
turning the key, the rain slanting down,
the wind playing havoc with a nearby tree.

Entering, often in the dark and
stumbling hesitantly to the pad on the
nearby wall, I punch the number in.
But should it be a three or a four, a five
or an eight? I've made mistakes before,
the alarm screeching, an intemperate
policeman rattling at the door.

On occasion too, late and exiting
flustered from the office lift when it
reached my floor, I'd fluff the entry code,
find myself locked out once more.
Won't someone let me in?

Those codes and pins so often have
me in a spin. Once it was undercover
agents and freedom fighters who
lived by codes, keeping out of sight,
transmitting clandestinely by night.
And those red-eyed boffins at
Bletchley Park, toiling to outsmart
their German counterparts.

And in earlier times too, the
Egyptians and Greeks with their own
secret signs, and Catholics smuggling
coded letters to a fated queen.

But now it's personal, and I'm at the bank
trying to get it right. The money may be mine,
but like misers they hold on tight.

Later, at home, I'm settling bills by phone
and online, or trying to. Credit cards, electricity,
gas, I need the pin, the code. Same with
the computer I'm typing on, the mobile I'm
calling on – different numbers, pins, codes.

Too much for one head! I'm tempted
to write them down instead, but that's taboo.
Still it seems the sensible thing to do.

And what code, I wonder, will let me in
to myself. A stranger still, I've yet to find
the way, to discover who I really am or
who those around me are. I've had time
enough, you might well say, but it's never
enough, and the going often tough.

Is it a five or an eight, or is it just too late?
I'll throw the numbers in the air, see where they land.
I don't expect to get a winning hand.

Coats of Many Colours

You'd be hard put to see them there,
those stately owls, though they are
there all right, their coats blending
perfectly with the forest's foliage.
Their call at night is unmistakable, and
when their razor-sharp eyes detect a
mouse or vole and they decide to dive,
their victims rarely come out alive.

Most animals seek protective camouflage,
even the most deadly, tigers pacing in the
long dry grass, stalking their prey, crocodiles
lying like logs at the river's edge waiting to
seize whatever unfortunate animal strays their
way, giraffes blending with the leaves of tall
trees, deadly snakes coiled within the brambles
beneath... and a whole arkful of other artful
creatures almost invisible against the assorted
backgrounds with which they merge.

And we too disguise ourselves as best we can,
masking our feelings, responding as we think
we should, wearing clothes to suit the company
we keep, piling on make-up, arranging
our hair, our thoughts, moving with care.

But when love strikes, celebrations call, or grief
invades, our cover is quickly blown as, vulnerable,
unadorned, we expose our true selves, if only for
a while, shedding a tear, spreading a smile, before
slowly reverting to the person others think they
know, arranging our persona, keeping up the show.

A Fly on the Wall

So many fortissimo conversations flying round
the room, everyone so fluent, so self-assured,
hardly pausing for breath. There must be a way to
intervene, though I've never really found the key,
as if words couldn't bring themselves to leave my
recalcitrant tongue just to make themselves heard.

I try my best to enter the fray, not to throw the
game away, but nobody notices, nobody really
cares. Too late I think of all the witty things
I could have said to turn a head, lapsing into silence
instead. I might just as well have been a fly on
those reverberating walls, not really there at all.

Yet sometimes I wish I could be there, unseen,
when words say what they really mean, at frosty Palace
breakfasts when royal indiscretions are fuelling the news,
when heads of state convene off screen, when plots
are hatched, when lovers confess and delicious scandals
brew. Now that's something I'd sign up to.

Eye to Eye

Every morning I meet his eye as,
with only a towel round me, I emerge
carefully from the small shower room
at the top of the stairs, almost shyly.

He's always fully and formally dressed
as he sits forward in a leather armchair,
a black waistcoat protruding through a
half-open dark jacket revealing his heavy
girth. His bright enquiring face is set off
by a short white beard, and a black skull
cap sits firmly on his head. His small
surprisingly gentle hands rest on his knees.

There couldn't be a greater contrast than
between the two of us, yet he was my
great-grandfather, that strong-looking
approachable man in the portrait that
hangs there in its Rembrandtian grandeur.

It must have taken him ages to get those
clothes on of a morning, given his piety and
the prayers he'd have had to say on rising
and the rituals he'd observe. And no doubt
his many children, ten in all, including my
grandfather, would have led him a dance,
knowing them all as I did and their own
idiosyncratic characters. It occurs to me that
I must be today about the age he was then.
It's hard to take that in.

I'm glad to have that portrait – and him –
hanging there under the skylight opposite
the bathroom door, on the only wall large
enough to accommodate him. It's so powerful,
so lifelike, that when my eyes hit his I wonder
what he's thinking. By all accounts he was a
cultured and enterprising man who, like
so many Jews, had fled Eastern Europe when
the pogroms raged, setting himself up in
Spitalfields as a picture framer and dealer.

I wish I'd known him. Some mornings I think
I detect a wink and wonder what he could possibly
think. Had we met, what would we have talked about
I wonder? Painting perhaps, for he knew many of
the leading arists of his day and would have had
a lot to say. And books too, but if he'd turned to the
Talmud I'd have had a lot of excusing to do.

Still, he seems to have time for me, that cultivated
man, and I hope we can continue to have those strange
early morning meetings at the top of the stairs, eye to
eye, come what may. I wouldn't want it any other way.

The Return

for Eilat and Yehuda

I was teenaged and full of wonder
when first I glimpsed Jerusalem's
magical hills, approaching them in
a packed Egged bus as humid day
gave gradual way to slowly spreading
night. However often one makes that
journey, it remains a thrilling sight.

By day, by night, I paced the city's
sprawling streets, marvelling at the
pinkish colour of buildings whose stone
seemed to have absorbed the light of
an insistent sun, and later at a sky so
bestrewn with stars it seemed unreal.

As I scampered among rocks and cypress
trees, ignoring the heat, it felt as if pages
of the Bible were strewn about my feet.

So often sung about, in both joy and
lamentation, Jerusalem may have endured
many conquerors over the centuries, but
the burnt-out armoured cars that lined the
old road from Tel Aviv were a reminder that
its history is not a musty one, and all around.

We were not then free to enter the Old City,
lost to Jordan by the fledgling Jewish state
in the war of forty-eight, and I would stare
down at its walls and ramparts little more
than a stone's throw away and at the rifles
pointing up at us. They looked like toys but
I was warned to keep my head well down.
I thought of David and his sling, of mocking
Goliath and the stone that felled him.

Visiting with my wife some twenty years
later, after the Six-Day War had brought
another bloody twist in the city's fate, we joined
the throng pouring through its now open gate.

The world beyond the Jaffa Gate was for me
an oriental wonderland – the scent of many
spices in the air, the rows of shops huddled
invitingly on both sides of the narrow pathways,
the Arab shopkeepers arguing and bargaining
with the tourists eyeing their colourful displays.

But for my wife, born and raised in Alexandria,
it was a familiar enough landscape, taking her
back to a childhood that had been snatched
from her but to which she would often return
in unsettling technicolour dreams.

This, though, was no dream, and I watched
in silence as she took it all in, a silence
broken by a muezzin's call to prayer from
a nearby mosque. We needed no reminding
that this was a city of many different faiths.

It was only recently, after many years, that
we returned to walk the dusty streets and
alleyways of this mythical city, and there
was tension in the air sparked by riots
and explosions near the Dome of the Rock.
Soldiers stood by watchfully, taking stock.
Steered by cautious Israeli friends, we strolled
towards the safer Christian Quarter and the
Church of the Holy Sepulchre, conscious that
some two millennia earlier Jesus had been
made to walk those same streets, staggering
along the Via Dolorosa under the weight of the
massive cross he was to carry into history.

Many who'd come before him and many
who followed had shed their own tears in this
fought-over land, and asked their own God
in their own tongue why he'd forsaken them.
But nothing could have deterred the pilgrims
kneeling in the church that August day, while
we, strangers, watched quietly from the aisles,
not wishing to intrude. Outside, waiting beggars
held out empty cups and young boys pursued
us, proffering crude wooden crosses, pictures
of the crucifixion and other mementos.

As intense as the relentless spotlight of the sun
were the emotions that swirled around us, and
with relief we stumbled into a small café, glad
to pause, drink freshly squeezed orange juice,
eat a pitta sandwich, have time to think.

Further along, the black-hatted guardians of a
different faith prayed in the open against the
surviving wall of their destroyed ancient Temple,
rocking backwards and forwards in their fervour,
lost to the modern world, and to many Jews too,
some of whom looked on, as we did, uneasily.

As much a Jew as they, what is it I guiltily betray
in writing this? It's not for me, proud of my lineage,
to judge or say, for who knows what they were
praying to redeem or what terrors they had seen.

Here the past, stoked by fear, is always
near, and there are many voices in the air.

*****

The hills of Judea that circle Jerusalem are
where the Prophets roamed, and still today
their peaceful beauty would seem to be their
natural habitat, timeless and far removed from
a world of tourist buses and impatient cars.

Gazing across at them, it's easy to imagine
a Jesus or a Mohammed, an Isaiah or a Jeremiah
emerging from the early morning mist and dew,
bringing to this troubled land the peace the politicians
in their parliaments and the holy men in their churches,
synagogues, and mosques have failed to do.

In this city of dreams, nothing is as fanciful as it seems.

A Fallen Oak

It's been lying there for several
seasons, felled by the wind, seemingly
untouched, children all over it.
It could have been sculpted by
a master artist, and perhaps it was.
No burial then, no chainsaws
dismembering it, no cremation.

It would have been too high for
those children to climb, but stretched
out now, a fallen giant, its great trunk
filling the wood's glade, leafless
branches stretching like massive
arms in all directions, it seems to have
found a second life, to have been made
to lie there, just for them.

How lucky to have been left like that,
for children to clamber over, for others
to wonder at as they stroll with their
dogs on their weekend walk.

I'd be glad to lie that way when
my time comes, forever staring
at the chameleon sky, welcoming
the night, the day, hearing the children
laugh and cry as I laughed and cried.

But no chance of that, the Heath's
regulations wouldn't allow, and besides,
the incessant rain and frost, and all those
three-legged dogs relieving themselves
all over me, would prove too much.

I'll take it as it comes.

That Night

I recall my uncle telling me that
on the night his brave wife Sallie died,
at the very hour, the great oak tree
that stood like a sentinel outside
the gate of their house for at least
as long as she had stood had
crashed, as if axed, to the ground.

Is nature so in harmony with
our comings and goings that
it fell that night in sympathy?
I hardly think so.

And yet there it still lies, spread out
majestically at their gate, in state,
while all around it brambles grow.
Waiting for what, I wonder? For whom?
I'd like to know.

A Birthday with Dylan Thomas

That moving poem you wrote on your thirty-fifth
birthday echoes in my head as I wake to a milestone
birthday of my own. You were no longer alive when
first I heard those flaring words of yours. Now I'm
over twice the age you were when you penned them.

Our bedroom window is shrouded in mist
as I move towards a day and date I don't really
relish. Your *Collected Poems*, a present, lies
beside my bed. No mustardseed sun to greet me,
no scudding cormorants, just the hoots and
hums of cars from the racing street.

The metaphorical ball you threw while playing
as a young boy in the park, might not then, as you
memorably wrote elsewhere, have reached the
ground, but why should it have done, given that
you were then still young? Did you wish it had?
Your poems teem with life, but with death too.

Given the time *I've* been allocated thus far, imagine
where any ball I might have thrown would be!
The luck, it seems, is very much with me.

We all know the story, the wild-boy behaviour,
the benders, the profligacy, and I doubt that you
would have been in a state to catch that childhood
ball even if it had landed in your open hands.

Yet your poems endure, and your transfixing
voice still booms from the records I continue
to play. But what a price you had to pay.

It's not a game, this life, is it?
Still, it's my so-called special birthday today,
so if I may I'll drink to you, to me, and turn back
those pages once again, wishing that in real life
it could be as easy to do the same.

Behind Closed Doors

All those champagne corks in the
rose beds, all those lipstick-tinged
cigarette stubs littering the lawn,
tell their own sexy story.

But later, upstairs, in another kind
of bed the exultant party guys will
have staggered to, expectant ladies
on their arms, they may well have
found themselves less able than they'd
planned to be, that the all-promising
fizz had well and truly gone, to their
heads no doubt if nowhere else.

Still, in the bleary morning, when they
eventually came to, there'd hopefully be
a new awakening, and from behind
closed doors triumphant cries of 'cheers'
will finally ring along the corridors.

An Afternoon Walk

I was alone as I walked in the park
that late January afternoon, or so I
thought – my mind a mile away, lines
and rhymes confusing my head –
when a passing lady stopped me
and joyfully said, 'Jesus is with you'.
She wished me a happy new year
and went happily on her way.

I looked carefully over my shoulder
but there was nobody there, nobody
with me, not as far as I could see.

The jovial lady was moving into the
distance now, becoming ever smaller
as she followed the path that edged
the surrounding woods, the sinking
sun illuminating the naked trees.

She was so sure in her message,
and I so taken aback. But still
I walked stealthily on, alone...
as far as I could see.

Leg Before

My eyes concave from watching
an enthralling Test and every bit as worn
as the ball they'd tirelessly thrown,
I felt in need of my own tea break.

The sun was relentless and the heat
at record height, so the nearby park
with its lawns and open space seemed
just the place to regain my head and sight.

And so it was, and more quickly than I'd
supposed, as my surprised eyes locked
on a woman lying face down, absolutely
naked, on the passive lawn of that normally
tranquil park. Such bare-faced cheeks!
Whatever she was thinking of, it wouldn't,
I imagine, have been of England.

Hard to ignore her, you'd have thought,
especially with a figure as enticing as hers,
but people were, men squinting out of the
corners of their eyes, smiling complicitly then
hastening on, mothers accelerating past with
their toddlers and prams, even the oblivious
squirrels continuing to play with their nuts.

But the two policemen who approached her,
helmets in hand, were not ignoring her,
summoned no doubt by an outraged citizen
of that bourgeois borough to do their duty.
But even they hesitated, conferring and moving
away at the last moment, for to turn her out
they'd have had to turn her over, and that, to
their relief, must have been beyond their briefs.

As for me, as I watched and wondered, I'd
forgotten all about the cricket, the score,
whether there'd be a follow on, a new ball, a draw,
and whether the batsman who'd been given out
just before tea really had been leg before.
It didn't seem to matter anymore.

Changing My Ways

Another summer escapes me.
I've spent too long staring at words,
chasing shadows, looking in not out,
while all about me life explodes,

flowers in their coat of many colours
performing their annual tricks, leaves
springing from branches seemingly long dead,
bushes crowding the surrounding beds.

They'll fade and fall eventually, but
return year after year, on cue,
as I can't expect to do.

From the window I watch a tiny bird
trying out its fledgling wings, its
first solo flight perhaps. 'Beware
the fox that lies in wait,' I hear
myself say as it settles on the lawn.

And what of the humans round me,
those so dear I sometimes fail to
see them standing there?

Looking up I perceive a smile I've loved
faltering in a way I hadn't seen before.
It's a warning call I can't ignore.

Life abounds and the flowers
continue their show-off rounds.
But now the landscape's changed,
become bleak, the sunlight dim.

It's clear I'll have to change my beat,
re-orientate. I only hope it's not too late.

Turning the Page

There was just a handful of boys
whose names I vaguely recalled, and
several others who later won some fame,
their faces etched in a timeless frame.

And there was one boy whose name,
hidden in a list at the bottom of the page,
was the same as mine. Curious, I turned
the page with care, for after six or so decades
it had begun, like me, to show its age.

There I read, amidst the results for
that year's boxing bouts, how he'd
entered the ring at seven stone three
and won a hard-fought fight. The weight,
the year, fitted perfectly, but still it was
hard to believe that boy was me, though
memories of a make-shift ring in the
cold school gym began to stir.

What made him spring through the
ropes that day I cannot say, only that
the school motto was Serve and Obey.

There were other mentions of him in that
old school mag, but none about which
he'd want to brag. Nothing scholarly,
not a single prize – hardly a surprise.

It might have seemed an easy ride, but
it wasn't always so. Behind those silent
classroom walls, and down those long
endless corridors, hidden terrors lurked,
especially in the perilous early days
when every foot one put was wrong.

You never dared be late or forget
a book, or talk in class behind your
hand. Those gowned masters may
have seemed way past their sell-by
dates, but most knew how to scream
and whack. It all comes back.

I turn the pages looking for further clues,
recalling the societies and plays, the
grey-haired masters dressed for Corps,
the morning roll call and prayers in an
echoing hall where names were read out,
either in blame or in praise, or because
they were no more. Hard to ignore.

I returned there nervously one Open Day,
hoping for what I can't explain, but there
was no one there I knew or who knew me,
not surprising given the years that had
passed and with them all the masters and
many of those who were in my class.

Clearly that boy I was is fiction now, just
a fading name on a black-and-white list,
and I'm no more him now than I am the
man I was yesterday, or the day before.
Just a stranger rattling a long-shut door.

In Its Simple Way

I love the way you've revived the
miniature wild roses I bought you,
lifting them from the white pot
they came in and soaking them gently
in the sink. It seems, as I often do,
that they were in need of a drink.

Standing there they looked so bare,
but back in the pot, in the centre
of our round kitchen table, they look
as good as the day I brought them.

As an alluring dress can enhance
even the most beautiful of women,
so the small white pot they're clad in
brings the deep red of their petals
to life, gladdening our eyes, bringing
in its simple way colour into our lives.

Game, Set and Match

for Caitlin

You're only ten, and not much higher
than the net. Yet you take those topspin
high balls in your stride, racing eagerly
from side to side untiringly.

I used to play that game, and proudly
display the occasional trophy that I won.
But you've already lifted many times that
number, and I stare at them in wonder –
and at you too as backhands, forehands
land with growing force and accuracy.

Keep aiming for the lines, serve deep
and to the sides, and when you're off
the court and facing other challenges,
remember that the one who keeps the
ball in play the longest usually wins,
and don't forget it sometimes helps to
drop them short and add a touch of spin.

Wimbledon Calls

Some will have queued for days, some will have
succumbed to the touts who circle the streets round
the ground like women of the night. Those in luck
will have won tickets through the official ballot
or their local club, or begun soaking up corporate
hospitality long before the first ball's struck.

Still more will be Mexican waving and cheering
on Henman Hill as the drama unfolds on a giant
screen, especially if there's a Brit to be seen,
rucksacks and hampers strewn at their feet.
For the royals in their box it's an annual treat.

One way or another they are finally there,
Pimm's downed, waiting for the umpire to call
'Play', hoping for a five or three set thriller.
They are out to get their money's worth, come
what may, not caring whether the men or ladies rule
the courts that day. The over-priced strawberries
and cream have to wait for a suitable break.

As if on a string, the balls shoot from side to side
with astonishing speed and accuracy, the spectators'
heads moving back and forth in harmony, like
pendulums in a clock, as they follow every shot.

They don't play like that at their own clubs or
local park, though some deluded ones might
think they do, their dolly serves and shots
struggling to clear the net, falling either too long
or too short as they puff around the court.

But now they are experts all, disagreeing with the
umpire's call, despairing when someone misses a
smash, serves a double fault, lets a tiebreak stall.

Back in the locker room, while the drained spectators
fight their way home, the losing players replay
in their heads the shots they missed, the ones that
clipped the net. All those hours of practice and training!
They know they should have won that final set.

Still there are many ways to serve and they've
signed up for this. Gluttons for more, they'll be back
on court the following week no matter where,
hoping for a kinder draw, to win a round or two,
to not come up against a high-ranked seed,
to encounter a softer player who'll concede.

The Governor

It might have been the formal attire,
the starched collar, waistcoat, the
perfectly arranged tie held in place
by a diamond-headed pin or perhaps
it was just the twinkle in his eye.
But whatever the reason, they called him
'Governor', and that he was, principled,
firm in his beliefs, at times austere.

Yet he was generous too, and beneath
that poker-faced exterior lurked a joker
in the pack who'd often take people aback,
unsure whether they'd heard what he'd
just said, or heard it right. Somehow he
managed to keep his smile zipped tight.

Yet behind the unexpected geniality, the
childlike pranks his Sunday golf partners
sometimes fell prey to, there must have been
an altogether different man we never really
knew, superstitious perhaps, serious to a T,
always insisting his family never wore black,
whatever the occasion. No arguing with that.

So when his own final day came, we honoured
his edict, arriving for that dark ceremony
in ordinary cars and wearing clothes that if
not gay were far from sombre, not a black
hat or tie in sight. We had to get it right.

And as, inevitably, his coffin was lowered into
the waiting earth and prayers were muttered –
his shaken family stepping forward one by one
to take the proffered shovels, add more earth –
he still remained in charge, the Governor he'd
always been, even in that final, dreadful scene.

Just One More Time

An evocative sound that stays in my head,
the steady ringing of the bell, the children's
high-pitched laughter, the organ-like
Wurlitzer music gradually slowing as
the merry-go-round came to a gentle halt,

which it did that summer's evening as I walked
towards it from the car park at the harbour's
edge, quickening my step when its flashing
lights came suddenly into view and the
steady looped music started up again.

'One more go, please just one more go,'
the children beg as they drag their compliant
parents towards the lengthening queue.
Always the same, one go never enough.
The ringing of the bell again, hurry, hurry,
the music reviving, the parents proudly
waving as their children ride by, some
waving back daringly. One for the camera.

How thrilling to be riding up and down on
the saddle of a wooden horse, clinging on
tightly as if approaching the winning post,
to be steering a vintage car or sitting in the
cockpit of a bright-red plane with spinning
propellers, dreaming of a cloud-free sky.

So real all this to them, and so transporting
for me, as the music and flashing lights revive
memories. I loved it then, and I love it now,
a moment of innocent joy and make-believe.

Night was beginning to fall as I turned away
towards the restaurant where my own family
waited, rather too old now to enjoy all this
though it was not that many years since they'd
been tugging at our sleeves, wanting just one
more go, 'please mum, please dad,' something
we laughed about that night and love to recall,
photos on the mantelpiece preserving it all.

High and Dry

I'm alone in a pub
at the edge of a lake.
To drink too much
would be a mistake.

From my face you can tell
things haven't gone well,
but to end up in a lake
is too chilling a fate.

So a small beer or two
will just have to do,
and maybe I'll join
in a chorus or two.

That she left me high
and very dry is why
I'm holed up here.
It brings a kind of cheer.

Still, I mustn't stay
and I mustn't stray,
well, perhaps a couple of shorts
to set me on my way.
It's been that kind of day.

There's gunfire in my head
and my eyes are bleary,
when I look straight ahead
I can't see clearly.

The sun has deserted the murky sky
as she has me, and it's about to rain.
All right, just one small one then
if you really insist, just to ease the pain.
I don't imagine I'll see her again.

Hanging On

Three score years and ten the bible gives us,
so clearly I'm in extra time as I edge towards
another milestone date, which they all are now,
and take a cautious bow. I've no complaints.

So far my ticker ticks on time and my hips
and knees are still all mine – no metal parts
as yet to set airport scanners ringing. I try
to watch my weight, am always slimming.

I'm hanging on.

True, I can no longer kick a ball around with
youthful vigour, nor wield a bat, and there's
no more rushing to the net or chasing
drop shots down – but who needs that?

In many ways I feel it's just begun and though
some things begin to fail I'm far from frail.
Thoughts still shake my mind, and pen in hand
I try to sort the lines and rhymes as best I can.

Admittedly I climb the stairs less quickly than
I did and gentle hills grow steeper by the day.
Can you repeat what you've just said, I didn't
really hear? You'll have to be more clear.

I'm glad to say the sight of attractive women still
excites, a litmus test that keeps my hopes alight.
My lady doctor says I'm doing fine, no wonder
I'm always at her surgery bang on time.

Yes, I'm hanging tightly on

not like an intrepid trapeze artist, swinging above
a gasping crowd, no safety net in view. No, heights
and daring feats are not for me. It only needs an
aeroplane to lurch and I'm clinging to my seat.

It's more earthly things I'm hanging on for, the smile
I wake to, the hand I clasp, the laughter of the growing
family round us, the books, pictures, songs we share,
the wonder of a breaking summer's day at dawn

of stretching sunsets in the evening sky, the flare
of lightning, the rush of rain, the first sight of
the sea, a childhood thrill that never leaves me,
the crashing waves, the wind, the salt in one's hair.

But most of all I'm holding on for you, for them, as
best I can, knowing that someone somewhere may
be hatching a quite different plan, that however far
from the wind I sail there won't always be a safety rail.

No Longer Valid

'Toss those notes and coins in the air,
that currency's no longer valid here,
nor anywhere. Might well be counterfeit.'

And so, it seems, might I.
To think I'd stacked high piles of
it away for a rainy day, staked
my life on it, checked it regularly,
thought myself secure, lived for it,
and now when water's racing in on
every side there's nowhere I can hide,
no one to provide.

I'll have to walk the streets, barter
all I can, plead, though when I tell
people about that worthless fund
I know I'll be laughed away, shunned.

I shouldn't have been looking just
one way, I see that now, should have
stored up more human kinds of riches.
It might have saved the day.

The Knock on the Door

Perhaps I'd devoured too many spy stories,
read too much about the Stasi and the KGB,
watched too many thrillers, or maybe it was
the echoes of a now distant war and its aftershock,
but awake or in recurring Gestapo dreams it's
the knocking on the door I'd hear and fear.

Yet this was no pounding on the door but
the insistent ringing of the front-door bell
startling me awake, rather earlier than
I'd have liked after a too-late boozy night.
Still, there was no dodging its commanding ring.
It might, after all, be good news in the post or the
parcel we'd been waiting for the postman to bring.

But no, standing there all smiles in the bright
morning light, a soberly dressed, mild-looking
balding man and a younger woman in jumble-sale
tweeds greeted me with the unwelcome words,
'Are you prepared for disaster?'

In truth I was prepared for very little, certainly
not for their easy words and practised smiles,
nor for the proselytising booklet they proffered
or the leaflets they offered. As politely as I could
I eased the door shut where they stood, leaving
them to speechify to the waiting blue sky.
It seemed the only way to salvage the day.

It was much the same the week before
when some grey-bearded elders from my
own parish rattled our targeted door.
I was not ready for disaster then nor even
redemption. Did I owe them respect?
Challenged like that on my own doorstep

I felt nothing but threat, shying away as
firmly as I could, as I always do, though
far more hesitantly than when local politicians
come a-knocking, whatever their hue.

Moving to the window, their unsettling
words still revolving in my head, I watched
the two fervent witnesses of Jehovah walking
unperturbed down our path towards the
kerb, smiling and no doubt discussing who
next to call on, who next to disturb.

Under Attack

Disturbingly, some bees have set up home
inside the crack of a beam by the front door
of the country cottage we've been staying in,
making it ever-more tricky to come and go.
Bravely, my wife has tried to cover the crack
with tape to stop them entering. But it also stops
them leaving, which unsettles them and us.
She's already had a nasty sting.

We wish them no harm, and can't bring
ourselves to use the lethal spray a helpful
neighbour has given us. It can't go on, but
we'll have to find another way to win the day.

A few weeks before, four foxes had settled
on the lawn in front of the back garden door,
very much at home, languishing in the sun
and climbing onto the round stone garden
table near the window, pacing round and round
on it and staring fearlessly in, as if challenging
us to emerge and face them down.

We continued to watch them from the safety of
the window until eventually, to our relief, they left,
perhaps to seek a more convivial stopping place.
We wish the bees would do the same.
Now when we emerge we do so warily.

And then early today, as I sat at the kitchen table
scribbling away, a sharp tap at the window made me
spin round, thinking someone had come to visit us.
But no, a giant bird had perched on the back of
a high-backed garden chair, its colossal wings
having hit the windowpane as it settled there.

To my unskilled eyes it looked like an eagle,
its large deadly-looking claws grasping the top
of the green chair. Startled, and not quite
believing what I'd seen, I grabbed my phone and
took two shaky photos, but only from the back
as it faced the other way. Finally, hearing my
movements, it stretched its metre-wide wings
and rose powerfully into the air, heading for the
nearby forest, leaving me to contemplate an empty sky.

We felt under attack. We'd only come for a short stay
and would be leaving in a day or two. But we'd be back,
wiser and more prepared for country ways, hoping the
bees hadn't multiplied, that no foxes ruled the lawn,
and that no circling eagles awaited us there at dawn.

That Fateful Day

Forlorn, leaving the hospital at dawn
after the last tearful goodbye, kisses
gently placed on her ice-cold cheek,
I find my car won't start.

There seems to be something with an
essential part. An act of sympathy perhaps,
and the second time that fateful day.

Summoned, a cheerful AA man brings
vital help and it coughs to life again,
as she could not do, despite the all-night
ministrations of the caring medical crew.

Driving away in the early light
I carried in my mind that final sight,
and it returned to me again just now,
years later, unbidden, breaking my sleep,
as it frequently does, repeat, repeat,
as troubling still as on that final day
she was spirited away.

A Lover's Lament

You no longer listen
to what I say.
You simply smile
and turn away.

There was a time
We chimed as one
Now what have we become?

For all too many months
the signs were there,
I should have been aware –
the raised voice,
passion's moments rare.

The days are slow,
the nights go on and on,
yet even if you greet
me with a stranger's stare,
I'll always care.

I call, I shout, shadows
at every turn, where we
laughed, where we loved.
I know you won't return.

The Elders

They were meant to last forever,
those respected elders with their long
gathered skirts and stiff wing collars.
Family was what they lived for, or so we
supposed, and their Faith was everything.
But who knows what demons haunted
them when curtains closed.

One by one they vanished from the scene,
as if gone on a forever holiday. Much
whispering in the wings and at family
gatherings, but for us, several generations
on, the seasons followed their customary
course and not much changed.

Not at first, anyway. But as the cast
at those gatherings dwindled we came
to understand an altogether different story,
felt somehow let down. They had seemed
so upright, so solid, so permanent.

Now we are the elders though we wear
different clothes, and the young now look
to us for the reassurances we once relied on
as we join in the fun and help as best we can,
and will until we too go on that eternal holiday,
hoping we've made our mark as those before
us had, but nothing sad.

That Time of Year

It's that in-between time of year.
Bushes and trees, recently transformed
into a magical medley of muted colours,
have had their final say, their autumn
regalia hanging by a thread, tattered
leaves smothering the surrounding beds.

The swaying lights in the streets throw amber
shadows on the walls as early darkness falls.
Books, ghostlike on the crowded shelves,
return my stare indifferently, no more the
welcoming friends I'd always counted on.
The pictures by their side do much the same.

Where once time dawdled, it seems to be
racing now towards an endgame with
an unknown dealer dishing out the cards.

These shortened days the phone rings less
and less, and when it does, cold calls at
whatever time of day or night have become
the norm, with someone selling services we'd
never want or seeking details they should
never have. More menacingly, there's
often silence breathing down the phone.

Letters tumbling on the mat are mostly
bills or circulars, while emails flowing at
an ever-increasing pace play a game
that's much the same these days, with
little there to set the heart ablaze.

Venturing out as drizzle soaks the quickly
fading light, I watch a seemingly endless
chain of cars and lorries hurtling across
the nearby flyover. Why the urgency,
I wonder? There can be only so many
candles on a cake, and we blow them
out as the years dictate. Who knows
how many remain to be lit.

Spring seems an eternity away, yet some
stubborn plants have lingered on, while a
lonely few have dared to face the winter
barrage down and show themselves before
they're due, though it may cost them dear.

But we can only applaud their courage, cheer,
savour these melancholy moments of the year,
take from them all we can, while waiting
patiently in the queue for our time to renew.

The Bride

A hush of expectation, the guests
now standing, eyes swivelled towards
the door as voices in the choir soar.

What is it she hopes for as, unable
to hide an expectant smile, she begins
her blushing passage up the aisle
towards the man whose life she'll share?

Deepening love, of course, and
he the same, and many healthy
happy years and hopefully a child
or two. Clichés all perhaps but true.

Vows will be exchanged, and also rings,
carefully chosen in an enticing store.
But are they the important things?
Vows may be disavowed and rings returned.
Who knows what the years will score?

Photos in the living room fix that
romantic moment, the veil, the smile,
the long elegant white dress, her
husband puffing his waist-coated chest.

And years later when passion may have
waned and disagreements hover in the air,
what is it that we wish them then, what
indeed do they wish themselves?

To be friends, true friends, whatever
the twists and bends, and at the last
stage too, that they realise those long
lost words were a blessing not a curse,
and they do what they swore to do

for better or for worse.

Against the Odds

It caught my eye that breezy
summer's day as I sauntered past,
a lone, blood-red poppy that had
somehow battled its way through
the low, white, jagged stone of our
neighbour's front garden wall.

That must have been a quiet,
solitary battle it had fought
and won, I thought admiringly.
Over how long I couldn't say,
nor whether in the years to come
it would return to the fray.

And yet somehow, for all its beauty,
its innocent tranquillity, that poppy
triggered images from an altogether
different battlefield, of soldiers deep
in mud, rifles raised, scrambling
over the top, of upturned carts and
cannons, the pall of smoke from
exploding shells, the rats, the rain,
the bodies lying where they fell.

As I replayed in my mind those
black-and-white scenes from hell
that flicker annually, in memory,
across our screens, the lone poppy
continued to sway in the morning breeze.

No bugle calls disturbed its easy
peace that day. No rose-tinted words.
No attack. No retreat. Just cars
racing down the winding street.

But then I saw, above that solitary
hero, two white butterflies circling
one another, rising, swooping in a
delicate pas de deux, bringing their
own magical tribute and salute,

making me feel suddenly upbeat
and resolute as they rose together
above the traffic's roar towards the
open sky and continued to soar.

Not Quite Right

That chair looks wrong from
here. I'll move it there.

That lamp is tilting
to the right, the light not
falling where it should.

That painting by the door
is far from straight, the figures
in the landscape appear
to be heading for the floor.

The globe on the coffee table's
upside down. Australia is
beginning to frown.

My glasses stare back
quizzically from the corner
searching for my eyes.

Outside there are fried eggs
on the Dali lawn and lawn
on the eggs. Is that the norm?

Is all awry, I wonder, or is
it me, and if so why and what
can I cock-a-doodle do?
It's not that I've been
knocking back a pint or two.

From your anxious glance
I can see it must be me,
but I can't just shift from
side to side, a little to the left,
the right, adjust my stance,
as if it were a kind of dance.

It's going to take far more
than that, and the careful
adjusting of a screw or two,
to see me through.

Passing Me By

They crossed me by the bus stop
one from the left, speaking into his phone,
one from the right talking into the air
in a language I couldn't discern.

From the non-stop speed of their words
and the urgent tone of their voices, someone
somewhere was waiting anxiously for those calls.
What is it, I ponder, that can't wait and why
proclaim it to all and sundry?

And when, later, they're alone with whoever
they were calling – in a restaurant perhaps,
or in bed together, will they have said what
they had to say, have run out of words, be
regarding each other in silence while hoping
someone would call, that silence saying it all?

I couldn't help but wonder.

After the Funeral

After the funeral, after the formal eulogies
the over-sombre recollections, we paused
outside to think about the man we'd just been
mourning, recalling the other person that
we knew, and had done for most of our lives –
prone to jokes, to laughter, to anecdotes,
stories from a life that had seen its ups and
downs, but one he'd drawn on to the full.

We all knew that there was a woman or two,
or maybe more, hidden away in his secret drawer,
and we'd heard about those nights out on the town.
For he was human, the man we knew, and now
he's gone we felt it only right to add a friendly word
or two, just between ourselves, you understand,
as we're sure he'd have encouraged us to do.

We couldn't let him down!

Do-It-Yourself

This is my crossword
do-it-yourself poem
I'll just
    scatter
the words

leave you to place them
    where you will.
        Enjoy the thrill.

Simply grab the ones you fancy
line them up (much like this)
add a dash of passion, loss, guilt,
think of the years that have
escaped you, the seasons too,
their fickle landscapes
the birds nesting, the frail
baby robins pecking the lawn.

See how easy it is!

Now think of the loves
waylaid, and the loved-
ones lost, the young
the old still in your care,
the anguish, the fears
the recurring tears

toss it all in the air
throw in a dash or two of
religious fervour
or dissent
to spice it up
as is your bent
and sexy encounters too
however spent

and while you're at it sprinkle a snatch of music
here and there, Beethoven or
the blues, as you choose.

But don't ignore the water
drip drip dripping from the bathroom tap
the steady knocking of a hammer
on the next door wall

the early-morning rattling
of dustbins in the street
breaking your sleep
driving you to the brink.

Might as well throw in the kitchen sink.

Don't blink.
Make the pattern as best you think.
Except I seem to have mostly
done it now myself, though
I only meant to hint.

Still it's yours, waiting there,
so stand it on its head if it fits the bill
go for the kill – you know the drill.

But remember this.
They're my words you're playing
with and I'm leaving them laid out
here, in trust, for you, so handle
them with infinite care, whatever
it is you decide to do.

Whatever the Score

Can there be lightning without thunder,
a horse without a carriage,
Darby without Joan?

I think of those whom history has
famously linked: Jacob and Esau,
Antony and Cleopatra, Abelard and Héloïse,
Romeo and Juliet, and, more comically,
Laurel and Hardy, Morecambe and Wise,
for laughter is an important prize.

Some names, some lives, are forever bonded,
as ours have been over many years, quietly,
off-stage, and will continue to be, whatever
life throws, whatever the score, until
time is called and we have to close.

from
*Thirty
Three
Poems*

Winter Fears

Shadows of a winter afternoon
  bruise the pillow where we lie
  losing desire in a sigh.

  Lying the long afternoon
Refugees from a nine till five
  nine till five existence
The future smug: home at six,
  too late for tea too tired for
  sleep for sex for everything
Sensibility frozen by routine
  by boredom, by the deadpan
  faces of the office walls, by a
  clockwork routine punctuated soullessly
  by pips and coffee breaks
My mind an unchalked billiard cue
  no poem written for two months
  nobody caring
  except me, lying beside you
  this unfriendly afternoon.

  Lying the long afternoon
  sensing distant shadows falling
  from the sky across the sheets
Desiring only to preserve desire
  uncertain whether I deserve you,
  the sun, or the countless
  comforts shunned each time they
  point conveniently towards me
Knowing only this is my house, a house
  like any other of these railway-line
  houses: wishing, pretending it were not
Knowing it a house like any other where
  fearful lovers lie counting their
  heartbeats, like us
  this unending afternoon.

An Evening Smile

'Be less serious,' she said,
smiling the enigmatic
smile I'd come to dread.

Soon parted – she to sleep
me to dream of sleep
and wrestle with the tappings
of the already restless morning –

I wonder if, after all, she is right and I wrong
to go on swallowing time, tasting nothing,
pulling its short rope towards me
like a galley-slave, hand over hand,

simply to meet the barrage of these evening smiles
and what is more, to try to answer them.

Man Alone

Betrayed, he nobly scanned
the ranks of new recruits,
resolved to catch a queen
to match his Anthony.

Alone, in lower mood,
he drank pubs dry
seduced whole streets
of easy women, wondered why:

later, ambling home,
declaimed to nightingales,
gave dogs on one-night stands
a knowing nod: man-to-man.

So help was always near
except when echoes pierced
the choruses of nights, and
whisky failed to deaden fear.

Then it was his time to write.

Letters to Algiers

No word. And to be frank
your silence swallowed
by the hullabaloo of Christmas;
such ballooned gaiety
(even the streets gay
in their own tinselled way)
all part of what we call
'the festive spirit'.
The swilling of drinks,
loud laughter and sly kisses,
then those winter-long hangovers,
and the loneliness.
No excuses.

Your silence quite unnoticed.

*****

Untrue. Untrue the news they flung
at me months later over drinks:
'Did you hear about Jean? He's dead.'
And then the dreadful facts enumerated,
acts I'd read about too often,
only comprehending with my head.
They'd waited for you while you prayed,
you and your sister,
in the old squat church that Sunday morning.
And then they'd struck,
slitting your throat and leaving you
thrashing like a fish, your mouth agape
in a final lost appeal.

And though the bells pealed loud and long
they pealed in vain.

This time all silence mine.

Why do we only hear
the clock's firm tick
when the clock has stopped?

Often in hurrying crowds
or hazy Soho cafés
I glimpse a face like yours, call
    your name,
but it's never you.
So maybe after all it's true.

And then again this year no card.

Fragment

He watched with fascination
the rain
pouring on our generation
and the clumsy plumbers
struggling to plug the holes.
As the holes broadened
pencils scribbled on paper
sums were done
wars were won:
the Minister cleared his throat
glanced at his notes
began to chant his speech:
'Twice two are four'
he said,
but the child smiled in disbelief
facts (he knew) were never true.

London Underground Scrapbook

Two eyes
stare back from
blank windows.
Whose, I wonder?

*****

At night
the low rumbling recedes
is superseded
by an almighty roar.

*****

I had quite forgotten
how many lovely faces
how many separate lives
roamed this lonely world
shedding identities.

*****

Always in a hurry
three-minute miling
along long corridors,
nowhere to go when they arrive.

*****

My ambition: to read
poems on the train
without everybody
branding me insane.

*****

He: what do you seek?
She: the last connection.

*****

Mad films, advertisements for firmer bras,
some kind of dream it seems.
'Four-and-a-half-per-cent for life'
'Learn Economics' end the strife.
Learn that demand exceeds supply
die securely when you die.
Sex is there for all to savour
(they're bound to have her favourite flavour.)
The Philharmonic will play at seven
make this your shortcut to heaven.
Theosophists declare that all are one:
we turn away and start to run.

Message

Always when shadows are darkest
when fear is loudest
when love seems most hopeless
you are far away
sprinkling precious water
over faceless deserts.

Pause a moment in your turning:
did you hear a heart beat one beat less
did you feel love falter?

If you did then hurry home
bombs are falling
sad leaves shroud the earth.
Not a glimmer from the faces round me
not a murmur from the friends I'd come to trust.

Silence has become too painful.
Leave the deserts, they don't need you.
Shadows fall and fear draws near.
Hurry, hurry. Let them find you here.

The Absences

At such moments
absence dominates:
absence of trees for birds
to hang their song upon,
of leaves for snow
to spread its fingers on:
absence of noise,
the restless traffic
finally at peace,
absence of time
as it resumes its unity.
Talk of war and rape,
ministers of state
screaming blinkered hate
across the pages –
all absent. Instead
newspapers talk of
mighty efforts
to save life,
encouraging us
to succour the old,
leave bread
for starving birds.
And they still sell:
survival has suddenly
become of interest.

Waiting in queues
and on platforms
people nod sympathetically
to one another – even joke:
children, kings again,
fortress the streets
with laughter.
Old and young,
the rich, the poor
kneel before one altar.
Snow's white flag of truce
strangles the city's roar.

Echoes

There are echoes we are forced to heed:

Shadows falling from the falling trees
dying voices of the leaves
tremors of the drying stream
the terror of the rabbits' feet
everywhere the shock of death, of birth.
These are the echoes of the earth.

There are other echoes we must meet.
London, 6 p.m.
Released, vast crowds stamp past.
Was it here that love held sway
(your suit blue, or grey, or black)
Was it here we made our pact?
Certain echoes won't depart.
These are the echoes of the heart.

Lights in a thousand pubs
the old refrains,
songs of the last war, the Great War.
Tipperary. Again. Again.
Songs that ruled our lives.

Will tomorrow's children
find these shadows at their feet?
There are echoes I fear to meet.
These are the echoes of the street.

The Departure

We spoke tonight
of the departure from Egypt
Climbing down the spiral of the years
Trailing our minds over the desert
Over the Sea of Death over the Promised Land
Over the might of Moses toppled
in the harvest of his field.
We sang tonight
chanting the ageless Passover songs
the memories of a People
crumbling the barrier of the years.

Over the cities of the world hung our songs
Over the abyss of the centuries hung our words.

We opened our doors
for Elijah, Elijah the Prophet
but prophetically he was forewarned and frightened;
they are all frightened
Prophets
Prophets are crucified
only Hitlers are heard
shrieking damnation.

And soon our songs hung silent
over the cities of the world.
Soon the tongues stood still
and the dust settled again
on the pavements of prayer.

While Troops Moved In

While troops moved in on
Berlin last night, we sat
in a car and talked
till the moon quit the sky.
We turned from the suffering
the phlegmon of war,
forgot the children born
with bullets for food,
forgot the girls maimed
by the dribblings of nervous men.
Like children we ran
through a fantasy world
where streams bred fish
not to be caught but to swim,
where birds flew fearless
in the trees below the sun,
and lovers sang of love –
not in the past tense, a lament,
but in a *now* of permanent fruition.
Laughter is the religion of love:
and we laughed while the world crept
to the edge of its perch last night,
and we sang and we died with the dawn.

20.8.61

Early
Uncollected
Poems

Too High

Must we be employed, said she
(meaning materially)?
We're employed by the gods, said he
they suck like a leech.
Our rent is high, said she.
High as the sky, said he,
and beyond our reach.

In Kind

The neighbours
wrote
'Don't
leave
your
litter
in our
street
not done'
the neighbours
wrote

(while
dead
leaves
spun
and a
stray
black
cat
excreted
down
their wall)

The Game

It was a game.
We made our rules
we played our roles
we mapped ahead
each move, each countermove.

We took the seasons
as they came: deafening
thunder, idling sun,
all the elements as one.
It was a hunter's game,
coiled fingers round the gun.

A game – no more –
the blaze of drums
a trumpet roar
our music splintering the air
the nights recoiling in despair,
...a lethal game
the wounds beyond repair.

The game grew pale.
With no set lines to speak
we drew apart.
We looked for other games to play,
heard the silence
heard the devil cough,
found the game we thought
we'd won was lost.

Finale

As always I recall
the last sad stance
on a stranger's stair.

Your flame-brown hair
no longer framed
a Mona Lisa smile
I knew, could touch,
trust, use as landmark
to reach distant ports.

Your flame-brown hair
no longer calm
but wild around
a marble mouth.

Two eyes of stone
blank words rehearsed
that reached their
heart and chilled.

Two eyes of stone
now left so dead
they could not shed
the final tears a
fractured love had bred.

One Weekday Walking

I stopped a beggar in the street
and asked him for some money.
    He looked down
    with half a frown
and dropped a silver penny.

I caught a copper in a square
and asked him for a statement.
    He spun round
    without a sound
and stammered in amazement.

I saw two lovers in a park
and asked them for enchantment.
    They drew apart
    and grew apart
and left me disenchantment.

I asked a dying man to speak
and cross me with his blessing.
    I saw the hearse
    and heard his curse
the last he'd be addressing.

Doncaster Return

for Deborah and Manuela

From his seat by the window an
all-knowing cleric announces his
congregants' faults to a faceless
young man, who blesses his words
with a series of Yesses and nods
of his closely cropped head.
The Junior Clergy, it seems,
aren't playing their part,
the Bishop's a bit of a bore.
So, by God, is he.
His voice echoes the wheel's
voice, monotonously sure.

Two girls, in facing seats,
cut in with views on knee-length
skirts, their college dance.
Opposite, legs crossed, a woman
in beige stares through the haze
her cigarette unfurls. Her eyes
speak men and many marriages.

The rain, incessant since we
jerked from Doncaster's side,
closets us. The fields aren't much,
little more than fuzz, hardly visible.
Eight minutes, by my neighbour's watch,
to go. My open book's untouched...

The girls are onto boys now
and a mutual friend who 'can't
sort herself out' – and gymkhanas,
ponies, the weekend's social round.
Our lady in beige uncrosses her
long legs meaningfully, exhales,
her mind clearly elsewhere.

The young man's nods have stopped.
Now suddenly, hands clasped, he
speaks, takes verbal wings, his voice
louder and shriller as his elder
gives him grace: his pulpit sways.
*We need more schools for the clergy,
the world's Godless, a disgrace,
we have a job to perform.*

Silently, stung, I beseech his God
to keep such 'helpers' from my own
new daughters. I too, I fear, have
a job to perform, rise, slide back
the door, peace gone, the real world
clear – lined platforms, distant queues –
and, nearer now, at home, the eager
eyes of two who wait their slapstick
father, clown, buffoon: whose laughter,
Yesses, nods, already call the tune.

Landscapes

I

It could be any city
and the Gothic church
at the water's edge
gives little away: almost
a stage set really
what with the neon sun,
the couple rowing, the
bridges, and the willows.

September: still a month
for echoes and longings,
though it's thirty-three years
since that war began,
but not today, not here,
only a couple, part of a landscape,
unconscious of time's dilution,
of the landscape of the memory
of a thirty-three-year-old man
who stands on an iron bridge
in a strange city, eyeing
a young couple rowing, a girl's
trusting head on her lover's arm.

II

I magnify, of course.
At the frontier, after
the shriek through darkness,
the autobahn's madness,
after the formalities,
the showing of papers,
we paused at the road's edge.

Two guards, tired no doubt,
bored no doubt, thinking no doubt
of their warm beds and the women
waiting, swaggered towards us.
As the car lights met their
holsters' gaze, their voices rose.
The Fatherland waits, can wait.
The trees ahead are crippled ghosts.
The engine coughs to life.
The barriers close.

III

A thousand miles away,
in a suburban London home, two
two-year-olds, back from the zoo,
speed towards sleep. The day's
events swamp their minds, and
'giraffe' and 'kangaroo'
is what they say. Tomorrow
their dad returns. They know.

IV

Along the red mile
the night club's signs
are the city's smile.
But the lipstick's smudged.
It's yesterday's party
and the drinks are stale.
The woman who takes your arm
as you saunter past, the men
who hover in half-lit doors,
have all seen 'better days',
and I have too, in a
film called *Cabaret*,
the Nazis leering in the swivelling
lights, the blood-red make-up
of the compère-clown.

'Is there more to see inside?'
asks a passing English girl, her
wide eyes drawn, despite themselves,
to the window's porn: spread-
eagled women and rising men.
There is – or was; but the images
burn and blur in the celluloid
light, and the ghosts return.

V

Anonymous behind a beer in
a smoke-filled room I wait my host,
who enters with two friends,
blonde-haired, my age: smooth-
tongued and charmingly they
speak of many things, of Goethe's
Faust, the poetry of Yeats.

Between their words a silence
stings – as do the laughter
and loud songs, the barman's
gruff guffaws, the cellar's
vulgar cheer...
of many things, and charmingly,
but my haunted mind's elsewhere.

There are confusing voices everywhere
until finally just two – small but dear –
break through, the message clear:
'Giraffe' and 'Kangaroo'.

Frankfurt, 1972

from
*Poems
for Jazz*

Song for a Season

Under a sun, under a moon
walk fast, walk slow,
and still the voices come
and still the voices go.

Rivers to the ocean
lovers to the war,
and still the waters freeze
and still the bombers soar.

Once I chased a shadow
once I stalked a ghost,
caught the voices lying
found I was their host.

And still the voices drum
and still the voices grow,
soldiers to the killing
driftwood to the flow.

A Face in a Crowd

I look for you in a crowd.
You are not to be seen.
Only a wave
Of salt-white faces
Images on a screen.
Someone distant:
Can it be? No.
A trick, a figment,
A simple longing of the mind.
Sudden panic. You won't come.
I feel the gap you'd closed
Spring open with the force
Which cracks when comfort
Tumbles from its cosy latch.
Then you appear.
Half an hour late: apologies,
A smile, a good excuse.
My longing turns to irritation,
And then to longing again.
An indication of my love's dimension.

On Track

Unlike the blandishments
of advertisements for toffees
that melt on the tongue
cough sweets that loosen, papers
that don't tangle you on tubes

Spring's unfolding,
red white or blue
or swastika black
sudden from tunnel
lining rail track
tenement
back to back
with council flat
wild by the manor

Spring's unfolding
skirts high
in the High Street
down by the river
recurring

Spring's unfolding
unlike, unlike I say
yet recurring
whistles
blow blowing
wheels rolling
repeating, the eye
the train skirting
council flat tenement,
the rivers retreating
the town from the mist
like a fist, returning.

Before Night/Day

It's got to be fast
fast
up in the air
wild and away
fast before
     night/day
     night/day
over the fields – flash – and away.

Away away away
over scarred meadows

(faster faster
the last sun falls)

away away
past sky/stream/willow
stampeding sky
stampeding stream
sad streamers of willow

(faster faster
the last bell calls).

It's got to be fast my love
and it's got to sing.
Sing. Sing. Sing.
Let your voice ring!
It's got to be fast my love
and it's got to win.

The ghosts are moving in.

Last Night

Last night was a night
of champagne and high kicking
and I strode that great hall
with a swaggering gait.
There were Liz, Kate, and Mary
in that raucous assembly,
and a Russian Princess
I had promised to take.

Yes, last night was a night
of fanfare and drum roll,
a cast of a thousand
all glitter and gold.
I watched them parading
like whores in the lamplight,
bejewelled and mascara'd
increasingly bold.

Then onto their necks
sprang the head of a monster,
instead of their laughter
shrieking and dread.
And into the room was
dragged a black coffin
and out of it stepped
a man long since dead

who greeted us all
with cheers and wild banter
embracing his wife,
his son, his black cat.
Then it all cut
to darkness and silence.
I woke up alone
the wrong end of the bed.

Cascade

Can you hear the thunder?
Can you *hear* the thunder?
My love
cascading towards you
in a torrent of hope.
It chases over
sun-drugged streets
at midday
over
frost-stung fields
at midnight
to breathe beneath your window.
Can you hear it now?
Perhaps the tone is too high
or the words too long
or perhaps the rain
has washed it away.
Don't go.
Listen, listen –
let me try my song again.

Blues for the Lonely

Now the birds begin to crow   It is the time for them to crow
Below them hurrying cars have almost reached their destinations
The crowded trains shrug slowly from the stations
Soon they will be gone   Only gaping stars lonely
and unwatched guard the sleeping city   The branches chatter
in the breeze   the grass softens under the falling dew.

For some there is sleep   for others only pitiless joltings
from uncertain memories   For some sleep comes in an
overwhelming cloud   hurrying them past smiling suns
to a Never-Never-Land of warmth and kindness.

But for most night brings a cover with cruel transparencies
So for me   It is as if a blind man felt suddenly for his stick
and there were no stick   or called softly for his dog
and there were no dog   There is no shelter no cloak
to hide behind   only question marks enquiring from the sky.

Seeing her spread contentedly beside you   you know for
the first time that you are strangers   and you know everyone
is a stranger   Desire changes to demand   You want
to run but there's nowhere to run to   You want to
shout but there's no one to listen   So you
pretend and smile shake-hands and drink and smoke and yell love
in everybody's face   And they tell you
you're a hell of a guy   and you believe them.

You believe them until you're alone   until you lie staring at
the silence   and the hundred questions illuminated in the sky.

from
In Focus

Just Call

You only have to speak:
I must respond,
move from my chair
to see to this or that,
answer you, refrain,
nod, shrug, explain.

The phone, at any hour:
I have to jump from sleep
to check that this one's well
that one free,
to say when we can come
when we cannot.

Raised voices on the train:
I'm soon drawn in,
lured on to speculate
how she would rate,
if he'll hold down his job, his girl,
if she, if he, if she...

Transistors blaze: forced to overhear.
Headlines stare: compelled to read.
Faces, voices, devils in my dreams: ensnared.
Call my name, sing your psalms, make your war,
speak your speech, Save my Soul...
Break down my door: I wait.

Back

Back down that street
avoiding the cracks in paving stones
vaulting high walls
ringing door bells
running
summoning hidden heroes
from behind trees, from behind hills,
D'Artagnan, Cassidy...

Back on that station
counting ten-second ultimatums
to expected trains:
not here in ten seconds
I'll jump, I'll scream.
Ten, nine, eight...

That high-domed room again
caught by the cracked prayers
of the shawled, swaying men
  We pledge this
  Deliver us from that
  Bring us peace Bring us rain
  Hasten our return

Back, smug conqueror, to that school,
that nightmare, jam-jar world,
now fictionalised, removed.
Same odours, sickening smells,
same names, desks, corridors,
same fears, rituals

  Let us pray
  Let us recall those colleagues
  Who gave their young lives

Same men, same masters, searching,
reaching back: 'Your name?'
'Were you here in...'
Ten years. Now back, unknown,
unrecognised abstraction.
Let us recall...

Tight-packed, queuing ghosts,
ten, nine, eight,
dust to dust,
gone, returned, pressing the nerves,
waiting the counting, the reckoning,
the long-knived, jackboot nights.

Reflection in Winter

Sick of it all, the whole persona: the smile
snapped to tame lips at his master's call,
lingering too long: the head nodding Yes
when the head thinks No: the issues let
drop, shrugged off, not worth the candle:
the whole damned manner too mild by far, a lie
masking a force coiled to breaking point.

Sick of being here, there, of the season's
fickle mood, of today's speech, tomorrow's
march, of the drizzle in the amber lights –
and most of all, sick of you my friend
yes YOU
your reflection there, cock-a-hoop,
smug in the store's dusty glass,
another cut-price bargain for men!
I shut my eyes: you're gone.
I turn: you're back the other side.

One day, I swear, I'll do it, unleash it all,
my umbrella raised just so – and
smash! handle first through the nearest
pane I catch you sniggering from.
Imagine the fuss, the salesman's stark face,
the Piccadilly traffic spun to a halt.
And imagine *her* face, caught
so off-guard, so credulous.

And in court, the friends lined up
to defend the man they knew.
Your Worship, truly, just a lapse,
a black moment, an urge, you mustn't think,
not for one moment...

No! Not for a moment.
Not of the noise, the pandemonium, glass
showered like confetti on this year's suit.
You'd only turn away, as now,
shrug it slowly off,
smile.

Waking

Waking, you said you saw your house,
the Nile snaking into mist,
Mohammed the one-eyed cook.
Somehow, you said, there were children,
running...

And I have watched you waking,
breaking from an Orient
half-hinted at in gestures, frowns
a craze for things with spice,
pepper, pomegranate, pimento, rice,
love of the desert, rock, the open sky.

And in you, grave refugee,
I catch an ancient plight:
not crammed in trucks
not stoned on sight
hounded by Inquisition
or crusading zeal,
but turned
without word without sound
from shore to sea: Suez '56 –
a Cairo-born French-speaking
Spanish Jewess on the wing.

It was wonderful, marvellous, you say
the late sun thumbing the Nile
the children running...
And away you go into dream:
the new London day dismissed
the four safe walls,
the friend that guards, regards you,
comes so close, retreats,
hearing a voice troubled in sleep
calling a new name, in a strange tongue,
distant and complete.

Moment

Here, in a corner of a world I cannot see,
I stand withdrawn. Buses and cars jerk by

nervously, past rows of shuttered shops,
bleak winter trees, past lights that blink

dutifully on-off, on-off, past me
standing in the doorway of a darkened pub

smoking placidly, waiting for the rain
to stop, the road to clear, waiting for you

to appear, or not appear, savouring
a caught moment of calm and no decision,

before voices stir, and the world stamps in.

Travelling

The Adriatic. Night. Lights
in waves of yellows, blues, and greens
ignite the trees: bats swerve between.
A random line recurs –
'Green the shadows in your hair.'
The music slurs.
The wine is sugar-sweet.
Campari grates.

*****

Urbino. Raphael's house,
alongside steep steps, guttered.
The mind, assaulted, notes,
notes first the lounge,
bedroom, study of the Master,
the lounge especially –
large, white, the place for nights
for reverie, where light decants.
Nearby, encased, five letters
from an English lord
who restored the place in '73
making it (to quote) accessible
to His public: a fresco
by an erstwhile host ignores.
The host has fled.

Outside, half a mile away,
the towered palace of Frederic the one-eyed
Urbino's patron Duke who gave the place its page
(at Pesaro Rossini's house was grave).
Two paintings stay like lovers on the mind:
della Francesca's *Flagellation of Christ*,
Uccello's *Profanation of the Host*.

*****

Travelling: the car exploring
mountain bends, blindly.
The brakes are dicey
and my hands tense.
Three hours and the journey's won.
On either side the Arno,
quicksilver in the sun.
Two ghostlike words accost
    Americani Assassini!
The accelerator's down.
Soon, Florence,
a room to kill the light.
The shadows on your lips are brown.

*****

And Florence: its famed Cathedral, marble
baptistry, chequered green on white.
Giotto's Campanile on the right.
Your arms are bare.
A pious doorman moves
to block our way.
A sharp exchange, and then we step inside,
go 'naked before the Lord'.
Angry, I note the arms of Christ
in Michelangelo's *Pietà*, bare.
The church is dark.
Your stomach pains
and migraine cramps my eyes.
We edge towards the day.

The shadows on Christ's arms were grey.

Let Those Who Come

Let those
   who come to pry
in private graves
   find only silent
willow
   and the granite's gaze.

Let those
   who run to lie
in stranger's bed
   find only silent
pillow
   and the stranger fled.

Postmark Venice

for Franco

Yes, friend, I remember.
You spoke of Lorca, and the space race –
'our future' you said, looking up.
I stared at the resplendent Doge's Palace
thinking 'leave me the past'.

Nostalgia, you'll say, but hell
what's it about, this struggle, anyway
if you can't sprawl in a gondola
clutching Chianti, howling
O Sole Mio at a Venice moon?

Why, they've even closed Rosina's
since '59, leaving a legend: Hemingway
in Harry's Bar would have raged!
No bordellos now – just tourists in San Marco.
'My world' you tell them – *O Sole Mio* –
and if pretty swing them low.

Here, in frozen London, another rail strike looms.
We feed second-hand on news.
Coups d'état, rocket ships, wars,
all passion spent elsewhere:
we hear and hear and hear.

Slip by the Basilica to your siesta
blow glass and cantos to a moon.
Reading your card, Venetian, recalling,
I strain to catch a wild Othello's cry.

Night Drive

That night, at 70,
the rain slashing the glass,
the wipers jerking furiously,

Beethoven's Violin Concerto
fought manfully to its climax.
And I thought, as the distant

lights revolved and I yelled
those final bars in unison
(so splendidly), how together

we could really make it go
the two of us – me with you, that is,
not Beethoven, a prisoner in my speeding

streamlined world, on at my will:
simply with you, locked in another
larger world. Yes, even at those

speeds, without brakes, radial tyres,
belts, another's work to rally to,
an easy switch marked 'off'.

Words to a Conductor

for David Atherton

I

The notes are there to start
though the art you give to them
brings pulse-beat, texture, voice
where silence was: the voice
admittedly not yours, but not

his either, quite, who wrote
them down. Your energies involve
themselves at will: tensions, doubts
compound. Last night's row, this
morning's tiff, the dash through

traffic in failing light, a
shirt too stiff, bow too tight –
all crowd, line up for the attack,
are stifled by the disciplines imposed
yet show. Words work less liberally.

Write 'black', the speaker's voice
says 'black'. You have a colour and
a social cause, Othello, riots, cool
Chicago jazz, must choose. Besides,
before you lift your pen you've scanned

the morning mail, stared headlines
out, answered four calls, switched on
switched off the news, a man from the
Electricity Board has called, you've
traded words, are bored, go out.

II

Hard hours later, and our set's
ablaze. You're 'live' from Albert
Hall, and the announcer's giving way.
Above the instruments' tense scrawl
a vibrant hush is rising to applause.

Outside snow drifts mysteriously;
a tree, raped of its branches,
stares vulnerably back, deposed.
The journey home today by British
Rail has been a babbling Hell

everything means something else.
The Overture breaks through, my tree
takes wings; the snow is somewhere
vast, Siberia perhaps, unrolls.
To tie this with a language that's exact

that *means*, is tone, is colour, shape
is all the things that you and painters
talk about, and more, is what we
try, and still you wonder why
there's 'nothing new' this week.

I envy you your abstract world, and all
that's caught in the music's swell;
a tempest or a nuclear war,
Napoleon's campaigns, a reveller's
sigh, pauper's curse, patron's snore

all there, or less, or more,
removed from the dictionary's stare,
the word worn thin by use, islanded,
abused, there on its own terms, refined
undefined, a baton's beat away.

Clubhouse Blues

remembering Vernon Scannell

It takes little enough, God knows,
a Teagarden blues, another treble-Scotch,
and stars come, not to 'Alabama' only
but to whatever rain-struck filthy sky is
dropping its abuse on the one, non-dry
patient county of England you're swaying in.

'I can't forget that moment, moment'
the record drools. Another glass, or
two, and – seconds away – you're up, wild
on your feet in a tainted, twisting world,
those tiny boring conquests multiplied,
alive in blinking lights, egging you on.

Reserve is gone. Two rounds, three,
'All comers taken willingly' you yell, as
stars jam down – on Alabama, Malvern, Cheam.
But the towel's already in. 'There's a poem there'
a far-gone second rules, comforting, limp,
as stars cut out, as crazy mirrors blink.

Then/There

The cash was slowly raised
one thousand down
twenty years to pay:
a house of praise.

We took great care.
Windows were cut
for light
to let in air

the stare of stars
broke, uniquely,
through fanlight
across the rise of stairs.

The walls of brick
proclaimed the strength of brick.
The floors
laid solid wood on solid earth

(a horseshoe for luck
at the head of the bed,
to the right of the door
a scroll of the Law).

And there
   the Miro
right
   of the mirror

defying the rain:
encyclopaedias to explain
that one and one, that one and one...

Scotch to pick you up
to lay you down:
the bric-à-brac of thought
books, paper, pencils, pen:
a clock that scored the years

and records play, playing, played
those jagged nights
when brick was solid brick
and earth was earth, and tiring
voices lost the will to sing.

Seen Again

Greatly maligned, because half-deaf,
he was the school's star turn,
the cunning ace up every joker's sleeve,
the mention of his name enough to draw

firm applause from the ranks of sour
boys he tried to teach. How we lapped
the stories up! One especially, of him
lying drunk and mascara'd in Soho Square,

flushed with lechery. Absurd, but we
believed it all, pointing and chortling,
inventing the semen's stain,
We gave him a name I won't repeat

hounding him with barks and yelps
quite openly. And when finally
'Where's that noise' he'd say, peering
left, we'd point the other way.

Tonight, spotting him after all these years
in the station's light, the same quiet
wife on his arms, it all comes back:
along with horror, shame, regret,

but admiration also for a stoicism he,
as Classics master, might accept.
And with this flares a loathing for
those other, surer men, who swooped

to bring back order when he failed:
who mocked him too, and doubly so,
by innuendo, sneer, and more.
Those relics of the barrack square,

bemedalled, dressed for Corps, raising
their sticks and egos readily
and physically at the faintest call
to mould a new generation of Cain.

Untouchables

The ones that get away
are the ones that stick,
catch in the throat like bones,
return to haunt and leer.

Often they are ordinary,
encounters on tubes or buses,
angry exchanges when the quips
arrived too lame, leaving me
to froth at mirrors, hopelessly.
Words, words, falling too slow
or too quick, ridiculous!

Or those in need of help,
the blind man injured in a street
because I moved too late, just
too late, too hesitantly...
Catches dropped, goals missed,
the timeless catalogue.

And women by the score,
plump women and slim women,
untouchables from cocktail parties,
the too-talls and the too-poised,
so often and so many

parading past like whores,
their breasts loose, their
buttocks swaying freakishly,
on, through my dreams
through the reeling mind,
down the shafts of sleep.

Pete Seeger at the Roundhouse

You brought us songs from the Spanish soul,
pure, loud voices of the peasant's labour.
Guantanamera: I am a truthful man.

From Little Rock, Montgomery, Birmingham,
charged songs of the Freedom Fighters.
We shall not, We shall not be moved.

From black German camps, Dachau, Belsen,
you brought hope, the human voice rising in song.
Up and down the guards are pacing.

In Turkish, Yiddish, Bantu, French,
gentle man, you brought us strength,
and on that stark, freezing night, a roof.

Night Final

Today's words
for yesterday's drama:
the embargoes on, the dock strike off,
the guns across the delta silenced.

Though the drama festers
yesterday's words, headlines,
interviews, are lost: the caught
killer silent behind bars, the grey
widow left to her own mourning.

By kerbs, under neons,
yesterday's cause, yesterday's curse,
now snatched by the late wind,
blurred by rain, left for litter,
as the frantic race hots up again, explodes:
tonight's news for tomorrow's banner.

Something Has Gone

Something has gone,
though the forked will of a tree insists
though used leaves smudge the lawn's edge.

November.
A man with his stick and Victorian cloak
has gone with jasmine and roses,

though the twin will of a tree persists,
the cold light of a sun splinters the lawn.
Something is gone.

By Taxi from the Prado

For 100 pesetas, in 'half-sun
half-shade' seats, we crunch nuts,
swig wine, complain about the heat.

The beauty's in the dance,
so the *aficionados* chant: watch
the stance, the speed, the body's poise.

Still in our heads, the Goya
dancers swirl: his firing squad,
caught in the night's storm,
stares down grey barrels,
his victim's arms outstretch.

Trumpets call.
Colours in the air.
Applause.

The startled bull stamps in.

Picadors, in twos and threes,
advance, tease on the bull, parade
spike *bandarillas* home, parade.

Colours spray the air. Applause.
The black bull backs away.
Drums roll – 'Matador! Matador!'
Protagonists must play.

Now the stance, the speed,
the iron nerve, the pas de deux
in which the bull will serve,

it's an 'equal fight'
but now the bull concedes.

And again the dance, the speed, the body's swerve.

Eyes confront, glory and death confront.

Just five in the afternoon.
The spent bull shakes
rises like a storm, and drops
as suddenly, its strength
legendary, its ears a trophy.

We turn away, believing the protest real,
the Goyas in our heads betrayed,
the churches' frescoes red.

Only real the carcass in the sand
and the stamping crowd's assent.

Rome, 90°

A city stuck with its songs,
marble palaces, and back-street whores:
three coins in a cracked fountain.

There the Arch of Titus, Emperor,
which Jews will not pass through,
Titus, Jerusalem's destroyer.

There the Colosseum, where Rome
watched lions tear, where creepers grow,
where furtive cats conspire.

There the Vatican, its golden cross,
and court, and silent kneeling throng.
We who are about to die salute...

There the Lancias and pizza bars,
the scented gigolos and rusting beggar's bowl –
there, and there! Arrivederci Roma.

Love's Lament

All the clocks
are telling
different times

    is is was
    and good is bad
    love is loved
    and has is had

today replete
today defeat
tomorrow yesterday today
the clocks repeat

Today I Go Left

Two ways to choose
and today I go left –
past the confectioners,
skirting the roadworks,
quick quick slow past the tower,
nodding to the newspaperman
clutching his dailies.
Today I take *The Times*.

Yesterday was different:
waltzed round (yes, *round*)
the square that time,
past where the car men
swear at the prices,
past the white 'home'
where, one spring day,
an epileptic fell,
blocking the pathway.
Yesterday, the *Daily Mail*.

Following, you'd think it odd
this ritual, this frenzied
search for new ways round,
once the staircase, rising
slowly, had spewed its cargo.

And listening, find it crazy
too, no doubt, this talk –
jumping the themes like hedges,
ducking fences, moving on, away
from, chasing the chasers.

Yes, mad too, the jockeyings
in bars, in bedrooms...
And those mixtures!
Bombay duck with cold roast beef,
Brubeck with Beethoven,
short-back-and-sides with a sage's beard...

Believe me, though, I've thought it through.
And so today, now leaves fall,
now summer in these concrete parts
has cracked, today, seriously,
snatching *The Guardian*, dodging a puddle,

today, as I say, I go left.

Destination

Walking the streets
I pace to find
some easing of
a troubled mind.

Somewhere there's
a meaning in
the miles of pavement
following.

Concrete shadows
edge away
towards a sky
resigned to grey,

neurotic drills
repeat repeat
a name, the traffic's
crazy hooters do the same.

And in the end
it's clear what I must do,
and in the end
it all comes back to you.

from
*Poems out
of Israel*

Approaching Mt Carmel

Many had come before
and many would come after
trailing lost images.

But still it was timeless
the still sea around us
the still sky above us
ahead the white cliffs
stepping from the mist.

They say that never again
will you feel this way
empty as the empty sky
you stand transfixed.

Never again, they say,
patriarch, priest or pleb
never again the same.

Sketches of Israel

We went to the sands
at midnight to eat
fresh-baked bread and hear
the symphony of the sea.

*****

Stars became shoals
of silver angels
talking urgently –
but we didn't understand.

*****

In the confusion
of such surroundings
where sand is religion,
the sovereignty of
water is enthroned.

*****

Houses with orange
brick faces: always
balconies supporting
them like white belts.

*****

Roads were driven
excitedly by thousands
of wild-eyed trees.

*****

Parties same as anywhere.
Marble-hipped girls,
saxophones pleading
for release; whisky,
an empty bottle of wine:
hangovers same as anywhere –
medication by blue-eyed skies.

*****

Love, unrequited love,
like the scent of jasmine and oranges
hovers tantalisingly in the air,
a mixture of longing and despair.

*****

The fiery sun is swallowed
by the distant sea,
the day is overcome
and night declares its victory.

Another Place

'On a hill near Jerusalem an old man watches the planting of the Martyrs' Forest – memorial to the Jewish victims of Nazi Germany' (from a pictorial history of Israel)

An old man silent
on a silent hillside
where six million grow
because six million died

under low skies
burdened with grief
dug their own grave
laid their own wreath

star upon yellow star
stare upon stare
only a bullet
to answer a prayer.

Six million trees
in six thousand rows.
Because six million died
six million grow.

The Rabbis' Prayers

They say that in the night
you stole your way to parks
and public spaces to consecrate
ground for the ritual burial
of your people: that when the
catches on the guns snapped back
and eyes, Belsen-red, gazed
down the unfamiliar barrels, you
called upon an ancient God
who some say heard you.

There were other voices –
women who cried: My child must live.
men, lashed by memories, who cried:
These bones *shall* live.
And, around, the darker voices:
Drive them to the sea.

Stern, holy men: while you
made your midnight pilgrimage,
while pits were being dug,
there were others who came –
up from the desert south,
down from the green north,
who left warm lovers' beds, cafés
on Dizengoff, neoned Haifa bars,
who waited the word of a
one-eyed wounded man: Defend.

June 1967

from
*Blues in
the Park*

Final Set

I have to say
the serves aren't what
they were, the lobs
fall short, the drives
that grazed the lines
now dent the net.
The volley's limp, inept.

There must be easier
games than this,
where finesse and guile and
grey-haired wisdom score.
I need to change my style,
get off the floor.

The tight-jeaned girl
who meets my Romeo eye
on the Underground home
offers up her seat. That puts
me in my place! Depletes.

Still, I'll not give way,
may have to cheat, serve underarm,
up the pace, spin, call 'out'
when balls fall in.
It's not much fun, but no regrets,
I've had a decent run.

Back on court and serving
for the set, I swing
it wide, my favourite ploy –
it's back at twice the pace,
no ace, no joy. Can't win.

Time to bow out, that's
clear, but not without a shout.
'That shot, the one
you're calling good, you're wrong
the ball was inches long,
not even near.'

My set, my match, my day.
Applause.
What's that you say?
Can you really think it's yours!

Spring's Decree

I'm worried about the willow.
For weeks now it's been spraying
the still bright lawn with its pale dead leaves
while the surrounding amber trees,
lit by a low sun, cling tightly to theirs.
Usually it's the last to go.

From where I stand its once domed, regal
branches seem like broken twigs, skeletal,
doing as the wind bids. Will it come
back next year? Will the fact that
someone cares help it endure?

It's been a year of human loss, too,
and while love and care assuaged,
in the end they couldn't cure.
Am I reading something into this?

Soon, inevitably, winter will have its
unpredictable way. Will that sick tree
survive, regain its potency? We can only
wait for the seasons to turn, and for
omnipotent spring to issue its decree.

Vigil

I don't accuse,
am on my guard,
that's all.

I won't forget they tried
to wipe my broken
people
from the earth – no,
not them, of course, too
young, their fathers or their
fathers' fathers – not even
them, perhaps.
Be fair.

They might, who knows,
have been among those
righteous brave who
in reaching out their hands
sealed their own fate,
or simply those who turned
away, afraid. Perhaps.
Impossible to conceive
the fear, the shadows of
the night, the bootsteps
on the stair.

Now, a life-time later,
alone beneath the Bahnhoff's
amber lights, incessant
rain machine-gunning the
roof's grim glass, I tell
myself the hordes
I watch there, fighting
their way towards the waiting
trains – *achtung* – late for
work or hurrying home,

that they could not
themselves have heard
the shots, the muzzled
cries, the dogs, the
clank, clank, clank
of the nightmare trucks
departing on cue for their
one-way journey to Hell
(from which of these platforms
I wonder – one, two?)

and that looking back
aghast, perhaps, at those black
Wagnerian scenes, history
to them, however obscene,
that they, contrite perhaps,
would wash their hands
in innocence at night –
not, like some demented Lady
Macbeth, scrub scrub
scrubbing
to expunge the dead, as
those accursed others should.
Sins of the fathers
heavy on their head.
Be fair.

And yet, and yet...
It's seventy years since
that war began, but if
I, a Jew, scion
of that haunted race,
forget, who will remember,
and if none remembers, the
dead are truly dead.

I don't accuse,
am on my guard,
that's all.

Baker Street Return

'Aren't you...?'
he suddenly whispered
looking over his laptop
throwing out my name
...and I had to admit
I was, the very same.

He'd been eyeing me
since Baker Street in a
way he thought discreet.
Someone from my past
it seemed, but who?
As the personal nature of
his questions grew I tried
to find some kind of clue.

But then the name tab
on his case caught my
eye and the jigsaw pieces
of a school boy's face
fell slowly into place.

That was him, of course, that
old class photo, dark-haired
sitting to my right – a nippy
inside-left as I recall. Hard
to equate this well-dressed
grey-haired man with those
bellicose boys who raised
such hell. I'm sure he thought
the same of me as well.

'I never go back', he confided,
'hated the place, means nothing now.
They're all dead anyhow.
And you?'

And me? 'Not yet' I wanted to quip, but
'me too' I lamely said instead.
My stop at last. I wished him well
and waved a warm goodbye.
In a strange kind of way
he'd made my day.

But it's not quite true I told
myself thinking back as I
mounted the moving stairs
and voices, faces, images
I hadn't heard or seen for years
gate-crashed my head.

Disturbed, it seems the dead
weren't quite that dead.

In Good Stead

I wasn't much of a pupil, I must admit,
and he, stooped gentle man, was no great sage.
Yet somehow we stumbled through the Hebrew
alphabet – *aleph, bet... gimel... daled, hey*,
studied fading texts, and come the day
and 13 struck, I knew my party piece OK.

It was to hold me in good stead, and when
in time love wove it's magic thread and under
the chuppah, in wonder, we sacredly wed,
again the ancient words broke through:
With this ring, *betabaat zu.*

The glass smashed (*Mazal Tov!*) and you –
thank the good Lord – mine, how that old
teacher would have enjoyed the wine!

Now, on Festivals and Friday nights,
when evenings dim and the mesmeric
light of candles reigns, the familiar
melodies, letters, words converge again,
reclaim memories half-shed, a boy's
urgent words in an ageing man's head.

And when, dreadfully, dear ones disappear,
and I'm called upon once more to recite
that mournful liturgy, sad leaves shrouding
the waiting grave, no mention of death
in the prayer for the dead, those letters, words
are there again, though faltering on the tongue,
meaning temporarily astray, while
the silent language of tears holds sway.

No, I was no great pupil, but that kind old man –
now gone, no doubt, to the great *cheder* in the sky –
knew what he was about, never a sharp word,
never a shout. Searching the alphabet I try,
as those early years, unbidden, disturbingly stir,
to find the words to repay my debt, come
back to just these potent two: *aleph, bet.*

Full Moon in Normandy

Excitedly, you call me to the window.
It's 2am, and a spectacular moon is aiming an
eerie spotlight at the outstretched trees below.
The scene is set for an all-star show.

As sporadic gusts of wind grab them by the throat,
ghost-like bushes, bathed in white, dance a war dance
on the lawn. Our tiny pond has become a moat. Although
summer, the grass is wearing its winter coat.

To us it seemed a magical moment, heaven sent,
its spell still infiltrating the darkened room and bed
where, huddled together, we finally lay, quite spent,
our spinning minds continuing to fantasize and invent.

Wallflowers

Those defiant poppies
on the bank are back, amidst
the show-off blossom from
the cherry tree and the daffodils'
dainty pas de deux.

'Look at us' they seem to say
in their arresting way, 'we're here for
all to see, ignore our regal finery
and we might as well not be'.

It used to be like that at those
Saturday evening dances, the
focus of our teenage week: the
over-coiffed girls along the walls,
all fancy-dressed and 'look at me',
waiting to be asked; and we,
young boys on the town (or so
we thought), all brylcreemed and
silk-tied, standing back, dreading
a rebuff. Until someone dared,
and then we'd all rush in.

That last dance was the important thing,
moving closer inch by inch for the kill,
the thrill of a possible kiss or clinch
as you walked her slowly home, stood
uncertainly outside her parents' door.
But nothing more.
Such wasted opportunities!

Meanwhile, back on the hill, the sun
drops behind the darkening trees
and the poppies are taking their evening
curtain call, oblivious of the embarrassing
memories they had sparked, not waiting
to be asked, and triumphant to the last.

Last Stand

All that's left now is an old bay
window centring a high brick wall,
lonely as a widow. Nothing supports it.
It looks as if a sudden gust of wind
would send it crashing.

Below, rubble all around, a grey
rainbow of dust choking the air.
Ashes to ashes.

It's very like those pictures
of the war, except there are
warning signs everywhere you
can hardly ignore: Danger. Keep
Out. Demolition in Progress.

No such warnings then.
Now men in white helmets
soldier the place. No sirens,
no air raids, no white lights
igniting a threatening sky.

Soon it will be rebuilt, ad hoc,
to meet a developer's design.
Flats perhaps, an old people's
home, a bland office block.

Yet for all that, something seems
wrong, a grand old house nearly
gone, with all its secret history.

What love has been made behind
that darkened window, I wonder,
and what deaths, perhaps, have
brought their own devastation?

Drawn in, I watch a crane, high
as the sky, lift a massive concrete
block from here to there. No alarms.

On the face of it everything is calm,
but that wall, with its solitary window,
looks ever more vulnerable.

Still, for the moment, like a
theatre tableau, it stands proudly
there, deserving applause,
though we know its time will
come, and the curtains close.

Just in Case

That wonder conker always took the prize.
It wasn't just its size. Wrapped and stored
through winter, soaked in vinegar, I pulled
all the tricks it took to win, and time and
again bragging rivals would be left staring
foolishly at a dangling piece of string.

And whenever autumn winds attacked and
fresh conkers fell like stones from the giant
trees near the old school gate, and though it
was strictly out of bounds, we'd be racing
there like hounds once the break bell went.
The spoils were rich but the risks great, and
we kept a wary watch for any mean masters
who might be lying in wait... just in case.

A lifetime later, strolling alone along a gusty
country lane, the memory tapes spun suddenly
back as I spotted dozens of newly-fallen ones
lying invitingly at my feet, their abandoned shells
scattered open-mouthed among
the rain-soaked, yellowing leaves.

What varnished beauties they were,
what champions they would have made!
The schoolboy I once was would have
grabbed the lot, subjected them to his
deceitful wizardry, and I couldn't
pass them by now just like that.

Scanning them with expert eyes
I pocketed the biggest for old time's
sake, bagging a few more tempting ones
for luck. Then, looking furtively round, and as
a ghostly dusk began to settle on the place,
I beat a guilty retreat... just in case.

Handle with Care

What a colourful Monday
morning that was. Not because
war was declared or some
dictator toppled, not because
England finally got the Aussies
in a spin, or scored a startling
World Cup shoot-out win.

But simply because there,
on the floor, to the right
of the door, on the 8.20am
number 13 bus, at the foot
of the stairs, a pair of scarlet
knickers provocatively lay –
just what was needed to
kick-start the day.

Quite how they got there
and, most intriguingly, whose
they were – questions that
hung tantalisingly in the air.
This, after all, was a respectable
route, not backstreet Pigalle, not
the Folies Bergère, where a flash
of this or that was de rigueur.

Why take them down here?
With so much to behold, how bold.
Imagination starts to unfold.
Was she slim, was she tall, blonde,
brunette, a *grande horizontale*,
a femme fatale? When the wind
blows, won't she be cold?

Doubtless the worldly French
would have shrugged it off,
winking at one another,
knowingly. Some frustrated
Madame Bovary on the loose,
perhaps – and in sober, religious
Golders Green what's more.
Encore!

But no cheers from us, not on
that bus. Nobody exchanged
a glance, all looked the other way
askance, tiptoed daintily round,
exited swiftly into the welcome
street without a sound.

What, I wondered, will London
Transport do? Wear rubber gloves,
blow them up, handle with care?
Put them in a plain brown wrapper,
Return to Sender (wherever she be
after her late night bender)?
Place an ad in the local rag?
Lost, one pair of scarlet knickers,
owner sought. Apply in person,
bring proof where bought.

Anyway, no time to think of that,
must get on, there's a train to catch
a serious day to hatch, and
besides, if she's going to apply
I'd best make sure I'm back and
waiting there... or will my scarlet
lady spoil the fun, not care,
go out and buy herself another pair?

Taking Stock

Those musty albums must have lain for years
under the stairs. And what a rum lot of characters
they reveal, posing for eternity. But my,
how they keep their guards up high.

Those starch-collared ancients, were they
ever young I wonder? And those stately ladies
at their sides, with their floor-long touch-me-not skirts,
a hidden armoury of armour beneath – were they?
Who can tell. We know them only as Great
Uncle this or Great Aunt that, stern,
forbidding, formal as hell.

Yet think of all the children they begot –
seven, ten, a dozen, even more.
They weren't brought by the stork I'll bet.
And consider their names... Max, Amelia,
Manny, Rose, Morris (known as Morrie),
Girtie the Flirty, lovely Harriet.

Go back a little, imagine them human, imagine
them young, in love, cutting a dash, hot,
finding a niche when niches were hard to find
in starch-stiff Victorian England – especially since,
it must be said, mostly they were a foreign lot.

By and large, though, save for a few bad'uns
I could name, their dreams came right just
the same and they could proudly pose for those
puff-chested photographs in black and white.

What though, I wonder, would they say,
seeing us now, long-haired, be-jeaned, dusting
them down, we, the future they made love for,
built for, prayed for – but proud of them all,
come what may, and with them all the way.

Blues in the Park

The landscape changes by the day,
haunting our lives in many furtive ways.

It's not just the failing sun, the ghosts
of darkening evenings creeping in
that halts the step, not the steady drip
of leaves from widowed trees, great
oaks felled, the rows of shattered
flowers gunned down by feckless winds

it's not just that: a season gone, a
season lost with all its rainbow colours,
autumn's melancholy catalogue.

It's the human landscape, altering by
the hour, by the minute, that makes
one falter – the shrinking list of friends
you'd meant to call but never quite
got round to, the tables you can no
longer fill, the dwindling cast at
family celebrations, grave occasions,
houses boarded up, their owners gone
moved permanently on, letters
Returned to Sender. The litany of loss.
Grief always just a phone call away.

Walking tonight, arm in arm in
the park we love just before closing
time, shadows are everywhere.
Passing the animal enclosures,
the children's roundabout and swings,
the spread-eagled oak, we finally reach
the old Victorian bandstand from which,
one glorious summer Sunday, to
our delight, exultant jazz exploded.
'The Humphrey Lyttelton Band', a board
announced, and so it was. Applause.

A care-free crowd lined the surrounding
lawn, danced and jived as we so often
had to that same anarchic virtuoso, birds
taking fright as his trumpet soared.

Now, as we skirt the lawn's damp edge,
silence rules. The desolate bandstand
seems bereft, no trumpet beckons,
no 'Bad Penny Blues', no 'Careless Love'.
Birds eerily line the wooden rails, waiting
for God knows who. Rain and darkness brew.

The landscape changes by the second.

Jazz at St Pancras

for Anthony Harkavy

'Play me' invited the piano on
the booming station concourse
and play it with brio the pianist
did, dodging the duff notes:
'Georgia on my Mind' as I recall,
which wasn't on many people's
that wet Monday morning.

Gradually, improbably,
St Pancras Station had started
to swing, with one couple clinched
in a dance and others gathering
round appreciatively.
A woman with a wobbly
voice began to sing.

Then slowly, as the rhythm
rose and the jazz flowed, six
tall young boys with grey college
scarves edged towards the
piano from the back, laying
careful hands on it in turn
as if the wood they were
touching was holy wood.

When, smiling, they turned away,
the large white hearing aids they
wore came startlingly into view,
and the amazed throng parted
for them like the biblical sea
of old, having witnessed the
surreal scene and understood.

Clearly, those boys had heard a melody
we could not, and suddenly the
station was no longer cold, and there
was more than music in the air.

Sins on the Water

Cast onto the water like that
will those sins sink or float, I
wonder, as I watch that ancient
ritual from a distant river bank?
And how will all those unsuspecting
creatures of the deep react
to such seemingly lethal bait
invading their private habitat?

Will they swallow them whole
(will the good Lord, Blessed be He?),
or will they simply nudge them aside
(will He?) as they glide through the
reeds that hug the river bed?
Mysterious indeed are the ways
of the On High, and of the deep.

Now, as another year turns, we too,
less observant but no less true,
must respond in our own way to the
continuing draw of the Days of Awe,
atone, begin anew, or endeavour to
as the Sages urge, though some we
love will have fallen by the way,
and there are wars and scars we
know the prayers of holy men won't
erase, even as we say, in whatever
tongue, All Praise.

Taking Me Back

for Carole

That was a magical walk you took me on.
What did I expect? Crocodiles leaping from the Nile?
The enigmatic Sphinx resolving its own riddles?
Cleopatra plying her seductive trade in the market square?

No, there were wonders enough in more earthly
things. Your hieroglyphic smile as we strolled that
memorable mile was every bit their exotic match.
So too the conferring elders, clasping
their hookah pipes in the packed cafés,

the rattling carts and kerb-side stalls,
the date palms and sycamores acknowledging
the breeze, pointing the way, the
intoxicating blend of spices in the air –
coriander, cumin, caraway, myrrh –
hot pitta bread, the scent of sand.
Everywhere the plaintive call to prayer.

The band of jean-clad youths who followed in
our wake, touting their wares, tugging at our sleeves, could
not have known this was, for you, a kind of pilgrimage,
childhood landmarks alive at every stage.

How often, in safe hospitable London, you talked
of this, awake or in sleep, and now here it all was,
a touch away, no longer myth. There, real as day,
masked by fig and olive trees, set back, your
family flat, giant geraniums trailing from the
balcony's rail. Next door, the makeshift
laundry-cum-store you would vividly recall,
steam still hissing from behind its wall.

Further on, the midday sun intense, your school,
and there, beyond the barriers, the famed
Gezira Sporting Club, less vibrant now than then,
where your sports-mad father Ben hit a vaunted
century against an English team – match won –
that was to stand him in good stead.

Here, on the expansive terrace, the oblivious ladies
sought the shade, drank tea, played bridge.
Circling it all, a racecourse where no horses run.
Excitedly, you find the pool where you learnt to swim.
So many memories to be taken in.

Later, after a siesta, following the tourist route to
the Pyramids, near the elegant Mena House
where you had your birthday teas, you laughed
to catch your English husband getting
the hump from a camel, falling to his knees.
Something you never thought to see!

Then, don't blink, across the mystic Nile,
relief from the heat, the historic ice-cream
parlour, Groppi, your childhood treat.
Turning back for more you caught your foot
on the uneven floor, stumbled into the street:
so many tantalizing flavours, hard to ignore.

Nearby, still there, its once regal facade
sulking in the shade, the cinema where, aged
twelve, entranced, you wept your way through your
first grown-up film, *Gone with the Wind* – and watched
your last, before being forced, in '56, to flee.
Gone, indeed. War's continuing history.

Night's all-encompassing mirage.
Despite the desecration – the pillaged gravestones
of Saqqara, the mummies staring into space
in the museum's large air-conditioned halls –
the darkness brings the centuries
back, restores their dignity.

Jackals howling, snakes uncoiling, with night
the desert too reclaims its awesome majesty,
stars splattering the vast Arabian sky,
while scorpions prepare their lethal sting,
eagles stir, and the mighty Pharaohs,
their curses heard at last, finally sleep.

A Small Reward

Those few small coins tossed into
the old guitar case at the busker's feet
are a small reward for the pleasure
unexpected music brings.

It might be a Dylan or a Beatles tune
that hits you as you ride the escalator down
making you want to sing, or perhaps a snatch
of Mozart, or a harp's melodious theme.

Today, in the rush hour, it was 'Where Have
All the Flowers Gone', fervently sung,
yesterday an accordionist playing 'La Vie en Rose',
touching off Left-Bank memories.

Mostly people stride swiftly by, averting
their eyes, embarrassed it would seem, but
often I find myself irresistibly drawn in.

Not all the performers are talented, or young,
and the screeches of wobbly flutes and shaky
violins also fill the stations' echoing corridors.
But some quite clearly are.

What, I wonder, could their true ambitions be.
Will that stirring tenor voice or finely modulated
cantata, that guitarist's flamenco lament or
jazzman's driving beat, eventually bring cheering
audiences to their feet with calls for more?

For the moment, though, they are ours, here
underground, shifting a mood, lightening the day,
and worth every carefully thrown penny, I'd say.

No Change

Fashions change,
but never yours.
With a beard and hat
like that
they'd spot you any day.
You'd never get away.

Vilna
Vitebsk
Stamford Hill
Golders Green.
Same old scene.

Times were
you'd have been
stoned on sight,
or rounded up
as you went to pray.
With those
sidelocks,
also, perhaps,
the stocks.

But not here, today.
I'd like to think so
anyway. For not
to be free is a
kind of blasphemy.

And though, like
those other cults and
creeds attired in
yellow, pink, red,
or burka-black
who grace our streets,
you often turn my head
even inspire a little dread
(I know you shouldn't
and wish you wouldn't)

clearly yours is a uniform
that's seen horrific days.
So who are we, in our
jean-clad, mini-skirted,
impious world, to wish
it, or you, away.

The Old Couple

On the dance floor, in bed, they know each other's moves,
it's all been carefully choreographed over long years.

And even if the mood is black, if something irritates
and an old unsettled score erupts, the cautious
words they use will have all been used before.
Nothing detracts or detonates.

Shadows of former hurts may lie in wait,
round corridors, across the floor, but somehow
they glide round them with no apparent show
he this way, her that, quick quick slow.

It's another kind of dance that has kept them
together all this time. And though the tune
may have vanished somewhere in the air,
the harmony they share is touchingly still there
complete, and beyond any conductor's beat.

A Doctor's Call

for my father, Joe

They seemed so magical at the time,
those giant round bottles with their
technicolour liquids igniting the glass –
red, purple, blue, dazzling green –
all plastered with fading white labels
and scrawled Latin words whose
meanings I could never glean.

Alluringly displayed in the dispensary
my father had alongside his surgery,
they were as mysterious to me as
a witch's brew, and even more
intriguing than the jars of humbugs,
gobstoppers, liquorice and more
that lay in wait at the corner store.

They were his own special mix
and I'd watch enthralled as he shook,
stirred, measured and poured the
strange-smelling concoctions, while
his patients waited trustingly behind
the adjacent surgery door. Amazingly
most came back for more!

A doctor of the old school, he was
part of their lives, knew them better
than they knew themselves, and they
loved him for it: half the cure, I'm sure.

And there was humour too. I fondly
recall the corny cartoons on the wall
behind his desk – a woman told to undress
replying, 'you first, doctor, I'm shy',
and a man, pointing to a urine bottle
high on a shelf, 'what, from here?'

Surgery over, he'd be off on his rounds –
in an old black Vauxhall, as I recall –
then back home for the evening shift.
More medicine poured, more pulses calmed.

When, seventy striking, he felt it time
to hang up his stethoscope, his bereft
patients hurried round, children in tow,
to shake his hand, many leaving small gifts –
wine, chocolates, home-made cake.
It seemed to him a kind of wake!

Then, fragile years later, on one indelible
day, his own faltering heart finally gave way.
Dismayed, I found myself surveying the drips
and tubes and the frightening battery of
machines they tried to save him with, and
thought back to those bottled cures of his.

Who knows, they may just have done the trick.

Still Life

A family's colourful history in photos old
and new stretches along the flaking walls
of the flat's long corridor – fading
formal portraits, bouquet-clasping
brides forever draped in white, children
knee-deep in sand, the waves rolling in,
babies, parties, festive occasions.
Smile for the camera.

But for all that, it's your tatty old hats
and faded woollen scarves still hanging
by the door, askew, that always hold
my eye – and that old stick of yours,
still showing signs of mud, as if you were
just back from an outing to the park.

Time to give them away, I hear
the chorus say, but no, I can't
let them go, for as long as they
are there, then you, for me, are
too, and every bit as real as all
those photos on the wall, and the
vivid scenes they movingly recall.

Who Was Who

Such deeds! Surely, no mere mortals could have
performed all these. Those daily obits of the famous
dead, whether of rogue or sage, read like fiction now.

How ignorant, how inadequate, they make one feel,
how captivating they unfailingly are, and the photos –
often black-and-white or sepia – add their own
poignancy; but the person's dead whatever's said.
No jobs to be got from those CVs!

Who's Who won't list them anymore, their
clubs will pay them homage with much grace,
then fill their place. They are no more real
now really than those many unsung others

who slipped more privately away on the
same black day: no medals to display
no great public deeds to salute, no works of
literature or art, peaks climbed, matches won,
life-saving discoveries, stirring symphonies.

Were they all really here? Indeed they were,
though writing of them turns them into history.
Just ask those dear ones left behind, bereft,
living in shadows, fighting back tears, photos
on the windowsill cataloguing the years.

Real, all right, they'd say, their impassioned
memories fuelled by love or guilt or even rage
and different in every way from those other
measured words we read and marvel at each day,
anonymous and distant on a transient page.

Some of Those Days

for my mother, Charlotte

There were days when fingers
stormed those fading keyboards,
but now, lonely by the fireplace,
that old Grand piano has no voice.

Somehow, though, it still retains its mahogany
dignity, covered as it is these days by a
canopy of family photos in silver frames
and the occasional flash of freshly cut flowers.

Frail now, but just as dignified, you sang then with
such pizazz, while my father, ever your accompanist,
raced behind you on those keys, all rhythm and bounce.

At the sudden memory of the impromptu
songs my parents would launch into,
and that sweet voice, my toes begin to tap –
'Some of These Days', your party piece,
as poignant and transporting as ever.

By chance, at an Old Time Variety show friends took
us to the other night, an artiste sang that song
amidst blue Max Miller jokes you'd have died for,
loving that saucy showman as you do.

Yet yours was the voice I heard, not hers,
and that old piano's too, striding behind, revived.
For my money, you topped the bill that night
and always will...
but oh, how we'll miss you honey.

From Time to Time

Some roots are easily dislodged –
a sharp twist of fork or trowel
and unwanted weeds go flying.
A number, more stubborn, demand a
larger fork or spade, fight a tougher fight
but in the end give way. A few
hang tightly in and win the day.

Part of nature's game, our own roots
are much the same, seem to be
shrugged off easily enough
until an accent slips, a slight hits
sharply home, a hand is raised,
a look in a glass betrays.

Even now, surprised, from
time to time I hear the Northern
vowels my father never really shed
and the even stronger accents
of his own parents – his pious Russian
father with his stern rabbinical beard,
his Polish-German mother forever
rattling off Chopin Polonaises on the
old upright as if nothing had changed.

Transported, I recall their rambling
house in Leeds where my father spent
his early years, the grandfather clock
at the foot of the creaking stairs,
and above all the deep coal house
by the black back door I always kept well
clear of, believing ghosts hid there.
I cherish them, those revolving scenes
I sometimes visit in my dreams,
and those vibrant voices, for though
distant, they're my voices too,
affecting all I say, and do.

The Party's Over

The fizz has gone, and those
abandoned bottles, coffined in black
plastic boxes in the street, give no hint
of the jollity they doubtless brought.
Like fish betrayed by the tide, stranded
on the beach, they seem to be staring
open-mouthed into a morning-after sky
way beyond their reach.

What the celebration was I'll never know –
a landmark birthday or anniversary perhaps,
or more excitingly, a lover's tryst?
Not my affair anyway, a stranger
in the November mist.

As if on cue, an old Cole Porter song
invades my head – 'French champagne,
so good for the brain'. Sinatra and Bing.
Imagine how many have gone down
to their seductive swing!

The band plays on.
Whether French or not, whatever
the brand, I tell myself, whistling along,
it always seems to score – skirts,
gowns, crinkled shirts and more
strewn along the floor.

As the music fades, the trees that line
the street, almost leafless now, seem
to embrace my meditative mood,
and the willow too at the lawn's edge,
contorted by the wind into a ghost-like face.

It's that time of year, and we wait
in limbo for the months to spring
their startling change, for the band
to re-assemble in the wings, for
bottles to be cooled, glasses charged.

'Another bride, another groom...'

Same old tunes, same old game.
We prepare ourselves to play it again.

Taken Aback

I knew these streets
like the back of my hand,
those shops, that well-kept
park, the wooden bridge,
the murky stream beneath.
This is where I sowed my
teenage oats on dark
Saturday nights when
winter shuffled in, suffered
embarrassing defeats, came
back again for more like
some punch-drunk pug
who won't hang up his gloves,
believes he still can win.
Illusion's constant tug.

Here I roamed on foot
where now I drive, ran for
the last bus home, wiped
lipstick from my lips when
luck was in, made light of
it when it was clearly not.
It always seemed like love,
but who can say?
How innocent those days,
the fumblings behind that
broken fence, the constant fray.

Long gone the dance hall
where we rocked around the
clock, shimmied, waltzed
and jived below the spinning
lights. Gone too the Odeon
on the corner where on
wet Sunday afternoons

we'd bag the back row seats,
planting a casual hand
on hers, stealing a kiss.
Now blocks of faceless
flats and late night
stores regale the streets.

I did not count on this,
following this route by
chance after all these years.
Pulling sharply up at the
kerb to take things in,
memories hurtle by, disturb.
I stare at distant doors
I once went through,
vainly search my mind
for faces, names.
Where have they gone,
where indeed have I?

I'm forced, it seems,
as insistent ghosts descend,
to meet it all anew,
pretend it's as it was,
be led astray – until, that is,
the red lights switch again
to beckoning green and
impatient hooters intervene,
break the fading spell,
propel me on my way,
make it aggressively clear
the make-believe is dead,
that there's an all-demanding
present to confront instead.

Close of Play

Out! The umpire's imperious finger
brooks no argument – leg before,
bungling a drive through the covers,
missing the bowler's spin.
I'd have much preferred leg-over.

The number of times I'd been
told, keep your head down,
eye on the ball, follow through...
but with so many mini-skirted wonders
on the boundary that day my eyes
were understandably elsewhere.

I'd planned to hit sixes and fours
all round the wicket, be the
centre of their applause and talk.
Instead I had to walk.

It only takes the sensuous smell
of just-cut grass to draw me back
to that school-boy afternoon, making
me endure once more the bowler's
jubilant cheer, the trek back to the
pavilion, the stark figure nought
jeering from a timeless board.

Those half-smiles and sympathetic
looks from the players' sisters and
their even more desirable mothers
in their clinging summer frocks
was not what I'd oiled my bat for.

Cheers should have been ringing
in my ears, nods and suggestive winks
the order of the day, covers of
a different kind teasing my mind.

Over the years there would be
many games like that, embarrassingly
recalled, so many times run out,
caught, bowled middle stump.
Occasionally, of course, I've had
triumphant times, won the day
(of course I have, I must have done)
but I'd be hard put to name just one.

Always it's the red-faced moments
that continue to haunt and flare,
any so-called successes difficult
to prove or maintain, impossible
to ensnare, never quite there.

That's the human game we play,
over after over, until the last ball
has been bowled, another umpire
calls a halt for fading light, and the
fragile bails are finally removed.

Hospital Notes

Tripoli's ablaze, and as chanting
rebels raze his Presidential compound
Gaddafi, like a rat, has gone to ground.
But here, within these four London walls,
another battle's being waged.

'I can't remember your name'.
When a mother says that to her son
it seems the end of the game.
We must continue just the same.

There's fire in her eyes as we ease
some food between reluctant lips.
She won't take what she doesn't like,
but then she never would! That's good.
We give her drinks she hardly sips.

When I crack a feeble joke to stay
her straying mind, she manages a grin.
'Cheeky thing', she says, and winks.
What is it that she thinks?

This, we are told, is a fight she cannot win,
she's old, her life's been rich.
We've heard those lines before,
it's a script we'd like to ditch.

She's been with us for all our years
and it's our turn now. We'll man
the barricades as best we can.

As always, my father's photo watches
from her bedside table. A doctor, he'd
be relieved to see her stable.

A kind nurse adds a little brandy to her drink.
She beams a smile again.
'*Le chayim*', we hear her quietly proclaim.
She calls me by my name.

A toast to life.
The mood's completely changed.
There's talk now of her going home.
She's sitting upright in a chair,
no longer seems deranged.

She looks towards the door. Born in
1914, she knows a thing or two about war
and will defy them all once more.

I raise an imaginary machine gun to
the sky to let triumphant bullets fly.

23 August 2011

Collage

Seven fifty-three, and as the bus heaves
forward jerkily, a collage of disparate
scenes distracts my still cloudy eyes:

the curve of grey rails on a white balcony
the redness of the bricks below, the way they overlap,

a fence over there that's lost its slats,
a grimy car in need of a clean, a
front door's sickly shade of green.

So many Shops to Let, Sales Agreed.

A dramatically tall woman in villainous
black stands at a bus stop, scarlet lips
igniting her powder-white face,

a dog has a man on the end of a lead,
two cats eye each other gingerly,
a snail has patterned the still wet street.

At the side of a run-down house, a
builder, cigarette in hand, leans beneath
his ladder brazenly, an empty bench
waits at the turn of the road.

There used to be a conductor calling
'fares please', but now a solitary driver
watches as the passengers coil in,
touch home their cards religiously.

Three stops to go.
My book, unopened on my knee,
stares back at me.

No angels hover, no star from the East,
my mind in free-fall now, released.

A Great Pianist Hangs up His Hands

for Alfred Brendel

That you'd decided to call it a day was bad enough,
the audience on their feet calling for yet another
encore as you took your final bow. No one wished
to believe your Odyssey complete
...or let you leave.

But today, in the silence of your London home,
you confess you no longer play now even for yourself.
Your hearing, down a notch or two, distorts the piano's
sound, the notes no longer true, intolerable.
You relate this over tea, philosophically.

For us, fortunately, the spell of your discs persists,
so we hear you playing even when you aren't.
For you, life's focus shifts.

You give master classes, work with
string quartets – the sound of the strings
still mercifully true – write, lecture,
give readings of your poems, distil
your thoughts... and afterthoughts.

All this you convey in your precise, fervent way,
and all the while your right hand seems to be
tapping out sonatas, non-stop, on your knee.
Beethoven would have seen the irony.

The Anonymous Man

I am the anonymous man.
I walk in shadows, furtively,
enter rooms when no one's there,
dodge the stranger on the stair.

I seek the cover of the night
hide my identity, keep out of sight.
Darkened windows draw my gaze,
and lamplights ghostly in the haze.

My complexion's pale, my
suit a neutral shade of grey.
My demeanour, mean, gives little away.
I fear the brilliance of the day.

If challenged, I'll smile blankly back,
adopt all kinds of cunning subterfuge
to confuse my inquisitor, get off the rack.

The eye I turn is invariably blind.
Ignoring this, evading that,
I seem to wear a stranger's hat.

I've spent a lifetime hiding all I can
I've yet to find out who I am.

No Answer

It snowed the week you died.
An early spring blessing
some would say,
but I'd rather there'd been sun
to warm you on your way.

Earlier there was mud,
everywhere, then rain,
shovels at half tilt. Is this
a joke you've played on us?
Can we begin again?

There's no answer
from the telephone
no one at the door.
However hard we call
we'll hear from you no more.

Ghosts and echoes fill the empty flat,
here the armchair where you always sat,
there the floppy hat you sometimes wore,
and in the dusty dressing table drawer
the fading pearls you kept for best.

It's cold, a window has been left ajar
and the evening breeze is snatching
at the curtain nets, petals spatter
the carpeted floor. Once full of song
this place is now an empty stage.
The piano waits, but the star has gone.

Night after Night

I've been on many journeys of late,
often dangerous, sometimes alone,
sometimes with haunting figures from
the dead, or else with half-remembered
others who appear instead. Night after
night they blast my sleeping head,
filling me with dread.

And who is that beside me now
calling the shots? I know the face
but can't recall the name.
It's always the same.

Why are we speeding too close
 to the cliff's edge – slam on the brakes!
Why are we adrift in this sky-high sea –
abandon ship, we're on the rocks,
the water's crashing in!

Who's waiting in that dark doorway,
who's that hooded by the kerb,
who's swinging that rusty chain?
My cover's blown, I'm on the run again.
There's a gun at my head.
I'm as good as dead.

There's a party raging round my bed,
the band's out of tune, their instruments grate.
I'm trapped in a surreal debate with people
I don't know in a language I don't speak.
Who are they all?
Whose voices these?
Why are they impossible to appease?

Almost Fatal

Not such a fantasy
sometimes, that almost
fatal urge, coming from
who knows where,
to do outlandish things
(while wide-eyed strangers stare)

to leap in front
of trains, pull emergency
chords, jump from tower
blocks, scream.
The compelling legacy
of dreams, perhaps, and
their mad imaginings.

Won't, of course,
despite the strong
mesmeric pull.
Too messy. Too final!

Besides, in the
queue other enticing
temptations brew.

To go two ways
down a one-way street
keep on the grass
not mind the doors

step on the cracks
of paving stones
ignore bad luck
tell a blonde
you know she's not –
duck!

at customs
declare your troubles,
faults, infidelities
(even your underwear)

stop when signs say go
run up the down escalator
embrace a nun
(what fun)
tweak a rabbi's beard
(how weird)

just once in a while,
in a fail-safe life, to dare
switch signposts round
make cars zoom
North
instead of
South

turn back Big Ben's
giant hands, delay
the News at Ten
make the nation wait
until you say when

ask a taxing taxi driver
for a tip, tell an unctuous
Maître d' his wine is off
that his haute cuisine
has turned you green
and when a stout
soprano shrills
(clearly over the hill!)
or a speech or turn
goes on too long and
interest palls, shout fire
clear the hall, have fun

not to cause mayhem
make them run
you understand, but just
to show one's flair
(because they're there)

irresistible at times –
almost – but of course
I never will.

Easier that way
I hear me say.

The Seventh Day

'...and he rested on the seventh day from all he had done'.
Genesis 2.2

What is it, I wonder,
that draws me,
a non-observer, so
readily in, time upon
time, on Friday nights
as darkness falls?

It's not the prayers
you understand, not
the twisted challah bread,
the wine, the candles.
Not simply these.

Nor even the ornate
silver cup that holds
the wine, the white cloth
covering the traditional
bread, embroidered round
the edge, the antique
candlesticks, the blessings over
this and that, the frayed black
book that guards the words
we say, its cover loose.

It's not just these, or not
only these, but the other precious
things they bring as well,

the friends and family with
us now, the family sadly gone
who prized and held all these
and passed them on.

It's also the Hebrew words
themselves (and not necessarily
what they mean), and this
timeless liturgy our forebears
clung to, even under regimes
that choked their liberty.

We do it all for all of them as well
as all of us, and bring them close.

And then, *Shabat Shalom* we say,
welcoming the Sabbath in, and hope
the peace the evening brings will stay.

Between You and Me

for my grandfather, Emanuel

Like sentinels we wheeled
you along paths, across fields
to a space beside a fence.
Everything you loathed was there:
grave clothes, grave countenances,

dull women in even duller hats,
the pomp and high-pitched
words you'd have topped
with a not-so-quiet aside.
Yet we were with you

all the way, your silent Tribe,
and when the clogs dropped
shattering the day, a bird flew
and something final snapped.

Moving on beyond the strangers'
stares, Shakespeare on my tongue,
Beethoven in my head, I knew
I'd find you there, not here,
amidst this black business.

One image sticks: a coffin
draped in a chandeliered hall,
mirrors uncovered, the usual
lights ablaze: to the left, poised,
a puzzled, watching bronze
and beside you, smiling down,

your favourite 'Dancing Girls'
their right legs raised.
As the service droned
I like to think you caught
their twinkling eyes, smiled
back true to form, winked.

At the Grand Hotel, Cabourg

This resort has clearly seen better days.
It was here the young Marcel Proust
dunked a 'petite madeleine' in his tea,
recalling its particular taste for posterity.
And here he later spent long summers,
à la recherche, at the elegant Grand,
writing round the clock compulsively.

Meanwhile, oblivious, le tout Paris, in all
its finery, paced the promenade by day
like figures in a beachscape by Monet.

Now the once fashionable hotel, all
marble and chandeliers, seems to be
waiting for a ball to start. In the empty
dining room a lonely pianist plays a
Strauss waltz, keeping his own time.
An elderly couple, formally dressed, edge
gingerly towards closed veranda doors.

Outside, a fiery sea spray, flung by the
wind, coats the windows of empty cafés.
The adjacent casino, where roulette
wheels spun through long smoky nights
while orchestras swung and the great stars
of the day – Piaf, Chevalier, Trenet – held
sway, badly needs a coat of paint.

But I love it here for what it is, and was,
the tang of the giant waves, the voices in the air,
the departed cast somehow still there.

The hotel lights are ablaze now and
six floors up, on an ornate bedroom balcony
facing the sea, a girl and boy are kissing fervently.

What would Marcel have made of this, I wonder,
as he laboured to rekindle his lost years
behind drawn curtains in the room the hotel
now flaunts as his, only venturing down in the
early afternoon, when the coast was clear, for
his customary Sole Normande and a café au lait.

Summer will soon be here, and it won't be the
same, towels and deck chairs splaying the beach,
children splashing in the sea excitedly, the
exploding sound of balls on wooden bats.

I prefer it now, like this, out of season, when
the only voice you hear is his, and all you've
ever known or seen or done is here for company.

In an Elegiac Mood

for Michael Garrick

We were supposed to
jazz that night, but
you didn't show

and when we learned
you never would
we shuffled the music
and did what we could.

But though the numbers
all carried your name
and the sympathetic
audience cheered
it wasn't the same,
the chords on edge,
the rhythm tame.

We knew it wasn't
like you to miss a beat,
but your heartless
heart had done just that
and brought defeat.

And once the word
was out, the final credits
rolled and quickly grew,
so many fine compositions
in the queue.

You were supposed to be
there that night, at the piano,
driving the beat, leading
the way, but another
conductor trod on your
solos and stole the day.

That last chorus should
have been yours, not His,
and all the applause.

11 November 2011

The Cartoonist's Glasses

for Peter Brookes

Borrowing his glasses to read the menu
I thought I'd get my own Private View,
that they'd reveal a flashlight world
of bloody tyrants and feckless politicians
where a pop-eyed prime minister and his
fellow schoolboy toffs held comic sway...
but all I saw was the dish of the day.

Of course it was his eyes I should have
borrowed, not his glasses, but they
weren't on offer as the wine was served,
his wit and wand hidden away in a
magician's cave, not yet ready to engage
and specially reserved – abracadabra –
for the next day's page.

Now and Then

I had opinions then on
many things, strongly felt, or
so I thought, and springing hotly
from the tongue, unsought.
But whose they were, and what the cost
and why they meant so much
is long since lost.

Now looking back, unmasked,
and as the ruthless years
exact their daily toll, it's
hard to know what role to play,
whose side to take, what cause
is just, what's really asked.

The eternal so-called truths
confuse the head, and mostly
are, I must confess, long dead.
I'd like to think that sure
but fading voice that now
sounds fake belonged to
someone else, a someone
on the make. But I can't
discard it quite, not yet,
though many of the 'wrongs'
I railed about seem right,
and many 'rights' scream wrong.

Holding back on different
fronts, diffident, less blindly sure,
may seem a coward's stance –
but not to me, with those years spent,
knowing now the voice that speaks
at least, at last, is mine, having
absorbed the bitter rules of time.

Lost for Words

I never quite know the words,
whether it's those rousing Last
Night of the Proms, Rule Britannia
Karaoke numbers the Promenaders
love to cheer and sing along to

or whether the potent psalms and
anthems I've known from ages past.
Somehow, however familiar, certain words
suddenly elude me, leaving me stranded
half way through, and God Save Our
something Queen just has to do!

Clearly, without me, there'll always
be an England, but nearer home,
when feelings swell, the caring words
of comfort, love, or hope that might
help wounded others cope somehow
arrive too late, or aren't quite right.

And even for you, the one who matters most,
whatever the praise, whatever the toast,
too often my litany of love falls short
as yet again my floundering thoughts distort.

I never really know the words.

Offside

You're on my right
I'm on your left, you're
confused, you say.
At home it's clear –
me left, you right.
But here, in this bleak
room, this cold hotel,
all's in reverse...
and getting worse.
Above us, footsteps
pound a creaking floor.
A toilet flushes in
the room next door.

A woman's operatic
scream, startlingly near,
brings us to our feet,
ends all hope of sleep.
Someone's thundering
down the corridor.
It sounds like war.
Amber street lights,
swaying in the wind,
strafe the mottled walls.

Outside I'd like
to think a wolf was
baying at a moon
but no, there's just
a barking dog and the
traffic's throttled call.

We could of course
swap sides
tread familiar ground
or better still
meet in the middle
make sparks fly.

But not here,
not worth the try.
Angry pounding
on the wafer wall,
makes that clear.

A kind of sleep, a truce
of sorts, descends
at last – until a rap
like a cannon blast
shakes the flimsy door.
You should have put the
Don't Disturb sign up outside
you roar accusingly.
Our early-morning tea,
ordered the night before,
lies abandoned on the floor.
Nerves are raw. Clearly not
my day, or night, for sure.

Best admit defeat
retreat, drag our cases
down the narrow stairs.
The lift's out of order,
nobody cares.

Hopefully the car's
still where we left it late
last night, not clamped
or taken to the pound.
Surprise! Surprise!
It's nowhere to be found.
The last straw. Language
soars. It starts to rain.

But no, my fault again.
It's over here, to the right,
just as you despairingly
maintained, not over there,
behind that bus, as I
adamantly proclaimed.

In silence, fists tightly clenched,
drenched, we retrace our steps.
Too late to voice regrets.

A parking ticket, triumphant
on the window, smugly waits.
Yet another fine to pay!
I try to force a smile as foot
hard down we pull away.

Anniversary

Opening the batting in those junior
school years, how I dreamt of
carrying my bat, scoring an heroic
hundred, or even getting a fiery
fifty on the board. It never came to
that, of course. Too many catches
edged to the preying slips or looped
to some grasping fielder on the boundary.
All those gruelling evenings in the nets
('attack', 'defend') brought little dividend.

But now, amazingly, there's another
kind of fifty on the board, though it
seems a myth. Aren't we just walking
to the crease, you and I, taking careful
guard, about to hit them all for six?

We've needed luck, of course,
nearly ran ourselves out on more
than one occasion, but so far,
mercifully, the third umpire has
looked the other way. Besides,
there's more than mere runs up
there now, and a strong family team
all padded-up to follow us in.

The freshly painted sight screens
may no longer shield the view as
determined bowlers race in on cue.
And while we know we'll never see
this hundred up we'll still play every ball,
block, duck, continue to eke the runs out
one by one as we have always done, as if
this were a match that could still be won.

from
Subject
Matters

My Valentine

You start a song and I continue,
I start a song and you sing on.
It only takes a note or two
for one of us to follow through.

There rarely is a tune that you don't
know, or words that make you falter.
That I am mostly out of tune and you
are not is something I can't alter.

It's a harmony of our own we've
somehow fashioned over years
not always filled with song, as
I've put this or that foot wrong.

Yet here we still are, hugging
and humming *My Funny Valentine*
all these years on from our first tentative
duet, your voice, thank the Lord of
Song, still going strong, as I think
thankfully back to the day we met.

The Performance

Whenever I stayed over I'd stand
mesmerised at my grandfather's elbow
watching him shave. An elaborate
performance, it seemed the old-style
cut-throat razor he used was never
sharp enough for him.

So invariably he'd begin by honing it
vigorously on a leather strop that hung
by the sink, talking to me intermittently.
Fleet Street's Demon Barber could
not have had a weapon more deadly!

After this came the shaving soap,
copiously applied with an ivory-handled
brush he kept on a small silver stand
beneath the bathroom mirror. Then
at last, eyes glued to the mirror, he'd
set to work, moving the blade skilfully
down his cheek, inch by inch.

Everything smooth, he was ready
for the new day, though not until he'd
washed and tidied everything away.

Now, racing through my own morning ritual –
ever-ready blades swiftly replaced when
blunt, the soap in its colourful canister
just a button squeeze away – I recall how
meticulous he was, how long he took.

But then, as an expert who dealt in objects
that were both delicate and rare, he'd
disciplined himself to take time and care.

I could learn from that.

In the Place Saint-Germain-des-Prés

The unexpected sigh of a clarinet
in the Place Saint-Germain and I was
back in a flash to my first Paris
odyssey and the jazz we queued for
nightly at Le Caveau, eyes always
on red alert for a Juliette Gréco.

There in that airless cellar I'd
jive with the best of them to the
Dixieland beat of Claude Luter, and
on one thrilling night to the soaring
soprano saxophone of Sidney Bechet,
his large ruby ring ablaze in the
spotlights as he hit the heights.

It was in the rather classier Blue Note,
nursing an overpriced pastis, that I
was to spot a motionless Bud Powell,
hunched head in hands on the floor, waiting
to be announced, waiting to pounce.

When he played, whether fuelled by
drugs or drink, his speeding fingers
commanded the keyboard as if his
life depended on it, as it probably did,
the spellbound audience shouting
for more. His virtuosity was like
nothing I'd experienced before.

There was exciting jazz too in the cafés
of Pigalle amidst the ladies of the night
earning their pay. They could give you
everything but love, but I was there to hear
some fine old New Orleans maestros play,
not to meet an enticing mademoiselle
and buy whatever she had to sell.

By then in Montmartre the party
appeared to be nearly over. There
was no Django strumming in the cafés,
no 'bal' at the Moulin de la Galette for a
Renoir or Lautrec to paint, and though
the girls in the Moulin Rouge could still
raise their sexy legs, could still can-can,
the thrill of a Mistinguett or a Josephine Baker
waiting in the wings to shock
and stir was no longer there.

It was in the chic Champs-Élysées
that I bought records by the great
chansonniers of the day, and to the
bouquinistes on the Left Bank that
I went to hunt down copies of Burroughs'
Naked Lunch and the unexpurgated
Lady Chatterley. Somehow I'd smuggle
them into prudish England come what may.

Nearby, among the dusty shelves
and well-worn leather chairs of
Shakespeare and Company, the
presence of Joyce and Hemingway
and the other writers to whom Sylvia
Beach gave brave and generous
sanctuary never seemed far away.

Back now this early summer Sunday
to the Place Saint-Germain, the sun just
visible through the leafing trees, the terraces
of the Café Flore and Les Deux Magots
still tourist-packed, though de Beauvoir and
Sartre had quit their tables long ago.

Opposite, the city's oldest church
seemed to be waiting in the wings, the
band still in full swing, the applauding
crowd indifferent to its history as a
girl began to sing, a hat went round,
and the saints came marching in.

Subject Matters

True, some might have gone mad staring at flowers,
bowls of fruit, fields, mirrors, dying too young in poverty
of unsavoury maladies; but think of the perks, all
those models queuing to be immortalised, all those
uncensored scenes, *Femme Nue, Femme dans une Baignoire*,
all those voyeuristic peeps behind the screens, curtains,
doors, dressing rooms, high-kicking cabarets.

And if out of sorts or running dry, they've always
had their own faces to paint, romanticised perhaps or
cruelly accurate: Dürer in Christ-like pose, Rembrandt
in old age, poor Van Gogh with his bandaged ear.

In early times too there were all those religious
masterpieces, on altars, church ceilings, palace
walls, commissioned by rich patrons eyeing their
own immortality: all-powerful Popes and Princes
commanding 'paint this', 'paint that', crucifixions
galore, and enough virgin births to fill God knows
how many Italian maternity wards. Sexy subjects
too – enticing Eves not giving a fig. Rich spoils for
the artists of the day, I'd wager, on top of all the
priceless beauties that came their way.

The witty configurations of Picasso, Braque, and their
experimenting contemporaries made it all more fun,
of course, and Pollock flinging on the paint, walking
over everything while others worked on abstractedly.
And that was before an unmade bed, a tiger shark
and a cow in formaldehyde took their bow.

So what can poets do that's new, confronted by blank
sheets of unhelpful paper – their pencils blunt, pens
out of ink, the phone, the front door bell ringing?
They'll just talk about themselves again, I guess, their
amours, broken hearts, lost youth, betrayals, death.

One thing's sure, there's not a lot to be got from
parking oneself in a field with pen and paper trying
to write 'trees', or 'flowers', or 'hedges', though
daffodils have had their moments, and poplars too.
And what would looking in a mirror possibly do
except scare the living daylights out of you?
As for the nudes, and those alluring ladies in the bath
that randy old Degas and the others liked to paint,
forget it, they'd only fling the soap at you before
you'd even raised your quivering pen.

Staring blankly now, as I do, through rain-spotted
windows, observing the forlorn trees bereft of their
summer finery, the headless flowers dead, the leaves
curled up at the lawn's soggy edge, the light fading,
I confess I envy them all their ready subject matter,
the exhibitions, the auctions, the freedom to do whatever
they dare, unimpeded by the dictionary's intimidating stare.

1939

Seemingly a year like any
except it was the year I entered
this world and learned to cry

except it was the year
a war began to rip that world
apart and tears would flow
from adults' eyes as well.
For millions it was an entry into hell.

My parents did their best
to play down what they could
but as the war progressed
I all too quickly understood.

Thinking back it is not so much
the candles on a birthday cake
that I recall, though these there
always were, but nightly explosions
startling me awake.

Vivid too are nights beneath the
Morrison Shelter in the cold front
room we scuttled to when the unnerving
sirens summoned. Would it have
saved us, I wonder, if we'd had
the kind of hit so many others took?

Mercifully, it never came to that
though there was carnage all around
and there were nights our own
house shook as huddled together
we fearfully awaited an all-clear
we often thought we'd never hear.

The radio in my parents' room
seemed always on, and there
was crackling and distant voices
they strained to hear. Even to
a child their anxiety was clear.
The blackened windows only
added to the fear.

I couldn't then have known
that just across a narrow sea
armies were marching, tanks
rolling, people vanishing.

Eventually, as horrific details
of the Nazi camps sifted
through, the reasons for my
parents' whispered fears did too.
From the many refugees they
helped they must have heard
first-hand their awful histories.

It's all a lifetime away now,
become fiction almost to a
generation fed on the films
of technicolour heroes shooting
it out dramatically on the big screen.
Yet the evidence is grimly
there for those who care.

Nightly now at home we watch
dry-eyed as the latest clash detonates
across our TV screens, shut ourselves off
from the screams of bereft mothers, fathers,
of children orphaned in a rocket's flash –
millions more still forced to shed
the desperate tears of war.

Will someone finally sound the all-clear?

They wait, as we did all those years ago,
clutching those they hold most dear.

Contender

Still hanging like trophies in our dusty attic
alongside my old wooden Dunlop racket,
those boxing gloves saw me through many a
bruising battle in our school's makeshift ring
as I strived to knock the stuffing out of an equally
determined opponent from a visiting team.

Now, in turn, it seems that they've had the
stuffing knocked out of them, the faded leather
sadly torn, the fingers limp. And no wonder
after all the blows traded as I waded gamely in,
the hours spent pummelling punch bags in the gym
and then time's stealthy haemorrhaging.

Vividly, as on a 3D screen, the scenes return,
the tense moments shadow-boxing in the wings
before being called to the ring, the gum-shield
slipped in, the grease, the sweat, the gasping for
breath as each interminable round unwound,
and then the second's urgent words in my ear
when eventually the bell did sound.
These were potent things.

Clearly those gloves will no longer trouble
anybody's chin, and that warped racket has long
since served its final ace, the strings frayed, a
screwed-on metal press its final resting place.

But a contender always, or so I'd like to think,
I'll continue to duck and weave and serve the
best I can, for just as long as I can say 'I am'.

In the Beginning

That large-format comic-style Bible
which came with bubble gum and candy
from across the Atlantic always took my
breath away with its startling colour
pictures and blood-and-thunder stories
spread across page after enthralling page.

Even now I can visualise those mighty
pillars falling under a blind Samson's
resurgent strength – the great stones
hurtling through the air, the terror of
the hordes who'd been mocking him
and of the lascivious Delilah who'd
betrayed and destroyed him.

Just as vivid was the story of Jacob
deceiving his dying father Isaac
to steal his brother's blessing, and
of Joseph in that flamboyant coat,
thrown into a pit and abandoned by
his jealous brothers in the searing heat.

And how frightening was God's anger
as he punished an evasive Cain for
killing his brother Abel, and how startling
his injunction to Moses from a burning
bush that blazed across the pages of my
precious book before my goggling eyes.
Nor can I forget those lions circling
Daniel in their den. Never had lions
looked so angry, so hungry.

These were stories made for Hollywood's
big screen – Moses angrily smashing the
stone tablets at his people's feet, the
massive walls of Jericho falling to Joshua's
trumpets, great Philistine armies put
to flight by a young boy's sling, their
mighty champion lying in the dust,
the vultures circling.

And what a merciless legacy of blood
and retribution this was, though at
the time I never questioned it.

II

Later, it was the films of Roy Rogers, King
of the Cowboys, that carried the day, and I'd race
to be first in the queue at the local Gaumont,
sometimes having to ask an adult to take me in.
There in the dark we'd roar and cheer as our hero
leapt onto his gleaming white wonder-horse Trigger
and galloped fleeing rustlers into the dust.

Gene Autry was the other cowboy who'd pull us in,
but for me Roy was supreme, his lasso spinning round
his head and pearl-handled pistols appearing from
nowhere in his flashing hands. Those were the days
before the burly John Wayne would barge his way
through swinging saloon bar doors looking for trouble,
his own fast guns ablaze.

But it wasn't just Westerns and the vast Texas
prairies that blew me away. There was Tarzan
wrestling crocodiles and lions in the African jungle,
swinging from vine to vine, diving from cliff tops,
and Robin Hood, whose arrows never missed,
fighting Nottingham's wicked Sheriff to the death,
swords flashing along the corridors and ramparts
of his castle. Scenes I'd watch again and again.

They were my magical heroes and I believed
in them all, together with D'Artagnan and his trusty
Musketeers and that elusive Pimpernel as well.
As real to me too was Biggles, whose aerial exploits
I pored over in eagerly awaited books that still
extend like trophies across a shelf in an upstairs
room, my name and address firmly inscribed
on the flyleaf in bold spidery blue ink.

Treasured too were the comics I bought
each week along with gobstoppers from
the newsagent at the corner of our street – *The
Beano, The Dandy*, and others – selling them on
at half-price to school friends as eager as I was
to follow the ongoing fortunes of Dennis the
Menace and Desperate Dan, supplementing
my pocket money with these ill-gotten gains.

III

Easy then to live in a world so removed from
one's own, so romanticised and make-believe,
so black-and-white for all the blazing colour.
But now, with too many dear ones gone and
terror spreading everywhere, the Bible doesn't
seem the stuff of comics any more, and comics
not the stuff of the world we see nightly on TV.

And yet it only took the latest James Bond
film to explode across our screens and the
boy in me was back for over two pulsating hours,
slinking furtively into an early evening showing
and cheering as enthusiastically as I did all
those years ago, when every weekday evening
at 6.45 precisely I'd be waiting there, impatiently
pressing my ear against our old Bakelite radio
while Dick Barton Special Agent took to the air.

But back now with the elegant Bond, and our
hero having blown the bad guys away and coolly
taken control, I exited guiltily into the protective
winter night, thinking about the racy cars, the
girls, the ingenious weapons he'd deployed,
and leaving the music to reach its own dramatic
climax and the final credits to roll.

Perhaps we need our James Bonds after all.

La Mer

She woke me with a song, quietly sung,
almost whispered, an old French classic about
the sea dancing along the glistening bays, and
how its silver colour changed as rain fell.

Entranced, I lay quite still, watching the sun as
it edged through the half-open shutters, holding
my breath, listening, not wanting to break the spell
as she sang thoughtfully on, as though to herself,
oblivious of all else.

To me it seemed that a memory was being
conjured from a distant French childhood long
lost, one I couldn't reach, intimate and all
the more precious for that, an enchanting way
to welcome the day.

A Poor Exchange

I knew him when he was Meadway
and her Speedwell, and there were
other pretty names I remember still,
Bluebell, Mulberry, Gipsy Hill.

We called them phone numbers
but all were prefixed by an Exchange's name.
Some, like Lords and Abbey, seemed to be
heaven sent, others like Balham, Brixton, Brent
more down-to-earth, urbane.

I recall some grand ones too,
Regent, Monarch, Seven Kings,
and even the odd artistic few –
Kipling, Wordsworth, Keats.
And there were posher ones for swells,

Sloane, Knightsbridge, Tunbridge Wells.
Often those hastily scribbled numbers
were a prize hard won as music slowed
and lights dimmed, but spinning those old
black dials for a date in the sober light
of the following day was a braver thing.

Of course it is the sexy-sounding ones
I remember most, Riverside, Field End, Mountview.
The butt of many a sexist teenage jest they
were rarely the ones that turned out best.

All are dehumanised into numbers now,
hard to retain, giving no hint of the voice
that awaits at the other end, whether
welcoming or restrained.

And all are stirringly visible still in the tattered diaries I came across recently under the stairs, covers worn, leaves torn, but continuing to enthral, as they wait wait wait for someone to call.

Mirror Image

We've been together now for all these years
and, to twist the old song, it's often seemed
a day too long. I've tried, God knows, but
still can't find a way to shake him off.
It's been a bumpy ride.

Of late it's become more than I can take:
the expanding waist, the stooping gait, the
one too many drinks, the back that aches,
the restless nights, the lack of care, the
tasteless jokes I've heard before,
those tired eyes that stare and stare.

Run though I may he's never far behind,
a darkening shadow stalking every step.
Whichever way I turn, he seems to bind me
in a tightening rope. He leaves me little scope.

When I look into a mirror it is him I greet
and less and less the face I want to meet.
That carefree laughing boy has long since
gone and deep lines crease the mouth and chin.

His hair, once thick, is now quite thin, and when
he grins that phony grin I too am forced to grin.
At times I'd like to smash that face right in.
But what good's that? Only the glass would crack.

For all this I'm kind of fond of him. He's been
here with me, for better, for worse, from the start
and not even death will do us part.

I Know I'm Jewish When...

...the unholy smell of bacon fills the air

At school it was always the returning day
after the December break, as those 'What did
you get for Christmas' questions were bandied
round the upper deck of a schoolboy-crowded bus.
I'd respond as best I could, but Chanukah
could never hold a candle to all this.

...a lobster eyes me from a neighbouring plate

Morning prayers were also testing times.
Faced with alien hymns I'd somehow mouth
the words, changing some to avoid the ones I knew
I shouldn't sing, for God, I felt, was listening in.
Clearly, a Pilgrim I would never be.

...I hear an anti-Jewish jibe I wasn't meant to hear

'But you don't look Jewish' was the surprised riposte
when, fists flying, I weighed angrily in, cheering
classmates egging us on as we wrestled on the cold
playground tarmac –until, mercifully, a passing master
firmly called a halt, realising it wasn't a game.
After that it was never quite the same.

...fresh croissants tempt when Passover forbids

In church for a celebration or commemoration
it's the kneeling moments when, while not wishing
to offend, I contrive not to bend, and when, if a
communion wafer is proffered, I shy quietly
away, anxious to avoid an unseemly display.

...Jewish graves have been desecrated again

It is not so much the beauty of the *Kol Nidre*
and *Yizkor* services on Yom Kippur, with their
echoes, shadows and memories, or not only
this, but also that indelible moment in an
empty Moscow synagogue when, led through a
half-hidden door by a nervous guard and standing
hand-in-hand with my wife and daughter in the
silent sanctuary, tears overwhelmed us
simultaneously.

...the echoes, the shadows, the Babi Yar memories,
the wary eyes everywhere as we approached.
So often the Prayer for the Dead to be said...

In Prague, amidst the gravestones of the ancient
Jewish cemetery, layered one upon the other over
the centuries for lack of space, the scholars,
the cobblers, the well-to-do ... in Cordoba too,
under a ruthless sun, where Maimonides' statue
ignites memories of a people forced to convert or flee –
my own wife's history ... and in the cobbled streets
of the Venice Ghetto, where the Doges decreed the
city's Jews must live and pray, as some do to this day.
Shylock might well think there is still a debt to pay.

Strolling in safer times as darkness embraced
the hills of Judea where the Prophets walked – the
vivid stars of a Jerusalem night like no other sight –
or gazing in wonder from the heights of Masada
with their martyrs' history, or afloat in Galilee's
beautiful Sea, miracles always seemed to be
near at hand in that biblical land
as they seemed to be again when hundreds of
Hamas rockets blackened those timeless skies,
though suicide bombings, beheadings, terror, gas
and rape continue to be the everyday language
of the surrounding states.

...there are calls for an academic boycott of Israel

Still the hostile voices that distort and abuse.
Do I hear the ghosts of history cry, '*J'accuse*'?

I know I'm Jewish when...

My New Diary

Remembering Dannie Abse

'Who's in, who's out?' you pondered
in your turn-of-the-year poem 'A New Diary',
echoing those chilling words from
the Yom Kippur liturgy, 'Who shall live,
and Who shall die' as God sits in judgement
on high and a new year begins.

You had your own painful roll call
to contemplate, as you began the
less godlike transfer of names
and numbers from your old diary
to the waiting pages of your new one.
Who has lived, and who has died?

And now this cold January day
I face my own new diary. Shockingly,
inevitably, your name looms first.
Of course, I remind myself, you always
were the first on lists, we joked about it,
and how your books (when there!)
were always tucked away, top left, on high
bookshop shelves, out of sight, unreachable.

A for Abse, and a number so often dialled.
I stare again at the old well-thumbed A page,
consider the unwelcoming new one.
I can't, I won't do that to you, old friend.
This year I'll leave the As in peace.

We'll start with B.

Lying in Wait

Back again, those two wood pigeons
seem to be at home on our lawn, waddling
in tandem like clockwork toys, pecking,
pecking at the earth at all times of day.
Woe betide any unfortunate worm
that happens to be wriggling their way.

They seem even fatter this year, and I
worry that a waiting fox might spring on them
from behind a bush, catching them unawares,
or even a cat. So I remain vigilant as I watch,
ready to make a rescuing sally if necessary.

But they don't seem bothered, so perhaps
I shouldn't be either, though sometimes
I see just one of them and peer anxiously
like a worrying parent until – relief – the
other one comes safely into view.

It seems there's always something lying
in wait that may prove fatal if seen too late,
or not at all, and there's no one waiting
by a window to unleash a warning call.

Out for the Count

It's a knock-out, they say, and a
knock-out it was that winter morning
when, tripping, I dived, eye-first onto
the tall iron gates at the end of the drive.

Coming round some long minutes later
on the cold concrete ground and as I
stared up, the threatening sky finally
ceased its spinning and the clouds began
to regain their usual ethereal shapes.

Confused, my memory a blank, I expected
at the very least to find a jubilant Ali spouting
and dancing and floating above me, as in
his glory days in Zaire, roping a dope, and
in that ultimate great Thrilla, in Manila.

But no glory for me!
Having been down for the count, the only
badge of honour I had was sprayed in black
round my bulging left eye, as if I'd really
gone those fifteen rounds. No pay day,
no second in my corner to pack on the ice
or fix the cuts, no applause, no high fives.

Slowly, I heaved myself up, swaying on rubbery
legs that didn't seem mine as I began to revive.
I should never have taken that dive.

Only Five Minutes More

There's a mother at the upstairs window
calling her son in, not too urgently and as if
she is expecting his plea for just five minutes
more to practise another shot or two at the
makeshift goal he's chalked on the garden wall.

It's a nightly ritual, a black-and-white scene
from another era. No urge then to rush indoors
and play on an iPad or iPhone or watch the
latest DVD repeatedly. Just another chance to
enhance his shooting skills is all the young boy
asks before giving in to his mother's demands
and final curtain call as daylight shrinks.

Like a *Woman's Own* cover photo from the '50s,
that pretty woman smiling and gesturing at the window
is a picture I continue to savour, recalling an innocent
time and all those miscued kicks of mine, but above
all that happy voice of hers singing a popular song
of the day which seemed to have been written
just for the two of us and we adopted...
'Give me five minutes more, only five minutes more...'
is what she sang.

Not much to ask, you might say.

You Never Know Which Way the Dice Will Fall

You never know which way the dice will fall.
I pledged to hold you tight and win the day.
If left too late it could be beyond recall.

A gambler's ruthless tactics may appal,
He'll look you in the eye then make his play.
You never know which way the dice will fall.

We seized our chance to answer love's rare call,
Dodging clouds, embracing the sun's display.
If left too late it could be beyond recall.

We've tried to keep in step, not let love pall,
Whatever the stumbling block, come what may.
You never know which way the dice will fall.

It's many years since we first set up our stall,
And there are debts I know I still must pay.
If left too late it could be beyond recall.

We've called the bluff of those who'd see us sprawl
And sent them packing in disarray.
We've always done our best to stand up tall.
You never know which way the dice may fall.

And It Came to Pass...

And suddenly, unambiguously, irrevocably,
it was revealed – There Is No God.

Newspapers headlined it, special news
bulletins trumpeted it, statesmen, scientists
theologians and all the religious leaders
accepted it. Signs had to be changed –
Services Not On rather than Services Now On.

But what would the religious leaders and
their minions find to do now, all the priests,
rabbis, mullahs, imams suddenly out of a job,
seeking redundancy pay-offs, looking for
accommodation, queuing at Job Centres?

And all the great old buildings erected at great
cost in God's name, would they be demolished?
To make needy homes for the poor, the beggars
on the streets, the refugees? And all the gold,
the priceless ornaments and embellishments
they housed – melted down, perhaps, to fund
ailing health and social services?

And what about the millions of murders
committed over the centuries under religion's
blood-encrusted banners, the continuing torture,
intolerance, cruelty? How would mankind atone
for this, and would discrimination suddenly cease?
Just because there was no God?

And that there is no God I know
because last night, in a dream,
God visited me and told me so.

And the word of the Lord is the word of the Lord.

Off to Ascot

His loosely tied tie doesn't match
and his shirt doesn't quite fit, but
that proud top hat still has a classy
ring to it, and his large black binoculars,
stalwarts of many memorable outings,
hang purposefully beneath a thrusting chin.

Curious heads may turn on the busy
morning road as he strides across,
but he knows it won't be long before
the riders are under starter's orders and
he's determinedly on his way, his wife's
embroidered dress and flowered hat
adding a certain dated charm as
she clings tightly to his dutiful arm.

Maybe this year, at long last,
those binoculars will see the horse
he's put his shirt on streak first past
the post, allowing him to restock his
wardrobe and raise a glass to his
loyal wife and the years they've lost.

Then, who knows, with God's grace
and a spot of luck, they'll be back
cheering in the stands next year as
the horse they've fancied surges past
the field on the final bend and they're
winners again, perhaps for one last
joyous time before they themselves
finally cross the finishing line.

Off to Lord's

Wimbledon over, they're on their way to Lord's
where the Aussies have already knocked up an
untoppable score. In their red and yellow ties
and white boaters, it's pretty much an all-male
brigade all right, scarcely a lady in sight.

Watching as they make their resolute way,
anxious to be there for the start of play, you might
well think them a bunch of old boys heading for
a school reunion, but to me they appear more
like jaded veterans of some distant war.

Eventually, whatever the score and as the
sun beats down, they'll decide it's time to
retire to the Members' Bar, where the talk's
of W.G. and the Don, of Hammond, Hutton,
Compton and other legends of the game.
Then, revived, they'll return to the fray,
unable to hide their dismay as yet another
English batsman gives his wicket away.

Veterans of many enthralling seasons they
can read a pitch as easily as they can a balance
sheet and consider themselves experts on
everything from tactics to spin. What need
of a third umpire when they can be called in?

But come what may they'll finally see the
Aussies off OK, though when and where
and whether simply in their dreams and
memories, with so much at stake that's
a declaration only the Lord can make.

End of the Year Blues

The days will slowly stretch themselves,
I know, and I've watched many winters
come and go through different eyes.
Nothing should surprise.

Once they were those of a raw young
boy cycling home in the evening gloom
full of promise and expectation, eagerly
awaiting summer's invitations, cricket
and tennis on seamless lawns, endless
seaside days, and, later, girls to cavort with
beneath the sun's fading rays.

And now these eyes have become those
of an ageing man, and each turning year
another hurdle, an unkind countdown
from a time whose end, one always
thought, would never come, too young
to care, illusion's snare.

Yet seeing dear ones vanish each fragile
year stiffens the resolve, reminds that
dark, light, dark, light is the way our world
revolves, gives you the will to fight on,
value all you have as, once more, the dark
dissolves around you, and light restores.

Thanks for the Memory

When he went, my father's old accordion
stared beseechingly from beneath the piano,
its black battered case held together by
pieces of old plaster and tape.

It weighed a ton, yet somehow he'd lug it
to the occasional party and all the old tangos and
waltzes would flow from it. To find the tricky
left hand chords, he'd put sealing wax over
certain buttons to steer his searching hand.

None of us knew quite what best to do with it,
so we left it for a dealer to take with other bits
of bric-a-brac. Regretting this, I guiltily rushed
to claim it back, but it was already gone –
for pennies I imagine, for a song I nearly said.

Now whenever I hear an accordion's emotive call
from street corner or station's echoing corridor
I think of him, his lips pursed as he played away,
and gladly drop some coins into the waiting hat,
doffing my own with thanks for the memory.

Fascinating

for Sam

Our young grandson Sam says he's long
been fascinated by the silver box on the
coffee table in our living room, and the
flaking cigars within. 'Fascinating,' he
exclaims repeatedly, as he lifts one up,
pretends to hold it to his lips.

They were my dad's I tell him, recalling
how my father loved to savour a cigar after
a meal, its rich aroma scenting the room.
But they are fragile now, I add, unsmokable,
which only makes him wonder why we've kept
them all this time. I often wonder too.

I can't explain that when I go to clear them out
something seems to tug at my sleeve from afar,
making me want to leave them as they are.
Instead I tell him they are a kind of memento,
confess, since he persists, that when a kid I secretly
tried a forbidden one, turned pale green, and hid.

'Fascinating,' he says, closing the lid.

At the Old People's Home

'Good to meet you,' he said, shuffling
towards me, thrusting out his hand.
'You too,' I echoed.

Down the corridor, a big sallow man
in a crumpled old suit was eyeing
me suspiciously, lying in wait.
His agitated voice made everyone turn.
'Are you my brother?' 'Are you my brother?'

There was no dodging his anxious question
or truculent stare, and I feared that when
I told him I wasn't his temper would flare.

But no, crestfallen he offered his hand,
hesitantly asked me my name and I
asked him his. I wasn't his brother
but I'd become his friend.

In a room nearby, a gaunt, fragile man was
singing a George Formby song in a high-pitch
voice, again and again, accompanying
himself on an invisible ukulele.

'I'm leaning on a lamp-post at the corner of the street
In case a certain little lady comes by. Oh me, oh my...'

A fair imitation, I thought, half wanting to join in.
He must have been staring at that open door
from his bed all afternoon waiting for that certain
lady, any lady, to come by. Oh my!

The layer of age between us was thin,
I realised suddenly, and getting thinner.

My new-found friend was back now, proffering
his hand again, calling my name, as people
wandered the corridor, some in dressing gowns,
entering other people's rooms, confused.

Near the entrance, a frail old lady on a small
wicker chair welcomed visitors imperiously
with a wave like the hostess she may once
have been, waving again when they left,

waving, waiting, it seemed, all day, every
day, and would continue to do so no doubt
until someone finally decided to shout 'lights out'.

Waving, we backed guiltily away.

Last Ride

It wasn't so much her black-gloved
hands clutching the reins, nor the
two gleaming black horses drawing
the Victorian carriage that caught
my surprised eyes while I dreamily
awaited my morning bus,

but rather the sexy pigtail that
protruded from her smart top hat
as she stood commandingly in
the spotlight of the early morning
sun, driving the horses on.

There was no coffin that I could
see in the pitch black carriage,
but since she and her seated
companion were dressed from
head to toe in death's uniform,
there surely soon would be.

Given the pigtail, the hat, the black
riding whip wedged beneath her arm,
I couldn't help but think she'd be
more herself in a chorus line or sexy
Paris revue, legs lifted saucily
in time to syncopated music. Who
was it she'd be calling on, I wondered.

The carriage was level with me now,
having overtaken the sluggish bus
for which I'd already raised my left arm.
Quickly, in case it was a signal
she misunderstood and I found
myself her horizontal passenger,
I lowered it, leaving her and the bus
to their separate journeys.

I'd wait a while till the next bus
came, preferring to travel in my
normal humdrum way. A good
deal safer like that, I'd say,
though if I had to be called on
I'd settle for her, any day.

From the Hotel Window

Unexpected, that ancient graveyard
stretching towards the hotel wall
and the medieval church behind,
its commanding tower and stained glass
windows catching the falling sun.

From the small latticed window of our room
in the old coach house hotel it looked like a
painting in the evening light. But come midnight,
and as I peered again from the darkened room,
a cold moon had created a different scene.

Now, the old graveyard seemed to have become
a shadowy place of ghosts and faint voices, the
grey tilting graves and the clumps of daffodils
that encircled them caught in the eerie spotlight,
unearthly, stage-like.

Any moment now it seemed the dead would
prise up those stones, rise gleefully from their
graves, infuse the silent place with life, put on
their own macabre show. Somewhere, I
sensed, an owl was waiting to swoop.

Fully awake now, watching, I hardly dared
to breathe lest I disturb their sacred communion.
Nothing would have made me leave the safety
of the overhanging room I spied from.

Had I seen what I had seemed to see?
Returning after a few hours of broken sleep
and as the early morning light began to wipe
the darkness from the window pane, everything
appeared to have been restored: the tops

of the old misshapen tombs encased, the
gravestones bowing even further towards
the cold earth, an all-embracing oak in the
background awaiting its leaves, the daffodils
swaying regally in their carefree way.

The dead, it seemed, now knew their place.

Bat Mitzvah Girl

for Lauren

Many years ago, in another century,
I took that same journey, as my own
father had and his before him and back
through the generations, mostly in other
countries under repressive regimes where
Jews were often vilified or killed.

For me it was a testing time, and even
before stepping nervously onto the *bimah*
in that packed, solemn synagogue to
tackle the ancient Hebrew texts, as I'd been
taught to do, I had to satisfy what seemed
like a *minyan* of white-bearded rabbis that
I was worthy of entry into Israel's House.
Miraculously, I somehow managed to.

You come now, the first in a long line of
formidable women from an old Orthodox
family to undergo this ancient ritual, and
you can be proud – even if it's not something
those forbidding Elders, deaf to time's
continuing chimes, would have allowed...
and in a service conducted by a rabbi
who is female too, what's more!
'Tut tut,' I hear them say. 'Oy vey!'

But have no fear. The daughter
of a Deborah need have no fear.

You always said you wanted to celebrate
this for what it was and is, not for the
presents, not for the disco (though I
don't imagine you'll be foregoing these!)
It's as if you knew that in answering this call
you'd be drawing the chord of history towards
us in an important way, enriching us all.

Reviewing the Situation

remembering Ron Moody remembering

I was at my best that night,
songs flowing con brio, quips
and sharp asides I'd never
used before. The spotlights
dazzled and so did I.

I gave them my Max Miller – 'Now there's a funny thing' –
my Groucho, Jolson, sultry Marlene, that smoothie Bing.
What a cast I conjured up, and then as laughter
and applause exploded from the 'gods'
I began to pick their pockets and let old Fagin in.
All together now...
You should have heard them sing!

They wouldn't let me go then... and you won't now,
or so it seems.

I sense I have an audience round my bed,
nurses, family, friends, shadow-like faces,
faint voices I can scarcely hear calling for more.
A spotlight appears to be moving in on me again
and the songs and banter swirl around my head
as once before, though nothing's clear.

Suddenly my voice rings out – do, re, mi, fa,
louder and louder, ghost-like, as if from afar,
filling the entire ward. Tra la la!

That startled them all right, me too, I have to say.
Somewhere I seem to hear applause,
though I can't be sure.

'Breathe in deeply, Ronald, let the music grow
my dear old singing teacher would declaim,
arms waving to and fro. So long ago...

My lips outline a smile.
I'm reviewing the situation.
Always the performer, I've never
died on stage, and won't start now,
not while there's still a show to stop.

So altogether then, just one last time,
let's take it from the top.

Out of Reach

Way out of reach above the bus stop
at the corner of our busy street, those
tantalising ripe cherries hang in bright
tempting clusters along the weighed
down branches, tempting the wind.

One by one over the early summer days
they'll nose-dive onto the indifferent street
to be crushed under our hurrying feet, their
blood staining the pathway, their stones
scattered like bits of fractured bone.

How tempting to come in the night
with a ladder or pole, but that might
be a mistake, not being ours to take.
Best let them be, another of the enticing
things not meant for you ... or me.

Up there they are showcased, not to
be intruded upon, not by us anyway,
and though for the moment some may
lie like spilled lives on the cold pavement,
unlike us, whose lives once gone are gone,
they'll return majestically each year
like a surprise, creating their usual stir,
and even further from our reach.

The Dream

It all started in a dream
You were walking down a road
There was a scream.

I tried to see which way you'd gone
But everywhere I went was wrong.
You were lost among the throng.

I found myself on a river bank with
Shrubs and reeds on either side
It seemed the perfect place to hide.

No sign of you there or anywhere
And if it hadn't been a dream
I'd have questioned what I'd seen.

In the city now at breaking day,
Lightning igniting the windows
Of buildings beginning to sway.

No chance of finding you here amidst
The maze of narrow streets as like
A drum the mounting traffic beats.

This may have started as a dream but
that dream's too real, no longer what it seemed.
Was it I who screamed?

Meditations on Giving up Work

I've walked away from a job today,
perhaps my last, but who can say,
and what had I lost as I stepped away?

Walking pensively out into the indifferent
street, an ambulance, a concrete mixer
and a removal van speed past on the wet
road, making me wait at the kerb's edge,
spraying me. Is there a message there?

The Thames I'd stared down on over years
that had quickly passed moved with its usual
relentless flow. I've seen its many moods –
treacherously calm one minute, angry the next.
Sometimes the early morning sun would press
the water, creating what looked like an illuminated
path, but I never caught a Prophet walking on it.

Opposite, on the other bank, the inscrutable
MI5 building would watch me arrive and leave each
day, giving nothing away, and Parliament's great
Palace, so clear now as I walked towards it,
would sometimes vanish in a Turner-like mist
rising from the water, and Big Ben too. Such
relief that would give me from its relentless hands.

Big Ben, my tormentor from my very first day,
had seemed to clock my every second as I stared
back at it from my office window. 'You and I will have
to make a pact,' I scribbled in a notebook early on,
but we never did. There was no escaping it.

The imperturbable statues I passed each day
would always draw my gaze, but won't be
missing me, for sure – a triumphant, horse-backed
Richard the Lionheart, his crusading sword
raised high, Cromwell leaning thoughtfully on his,
Churchill out-powering them all.

What would he make of the minnows who
packed that House now, with their laptops and
iPhones, I wonder, his presence commanding
the square as he stares judgmentally across.

I've had a lifetime of this to and fro, the smiles
that think they please, the daily crush on the
morning bus, up down, up down the unfolding
escalators, then back again in the evening rush.
A mind can only take so much.

Of course I'm sad, thinking back to the many
exciting times we had, though there were down
times too, winners and losers in the queue.
But every step away is a forward step, and
I refuse to see it any other way.

Inside the station now, someone is playing
Chagrin d'Amour on a clarinet, beautifully,
the mood of that lovely song chiming perfectly
with mine. A man has not lived who has not
felt love's tug, I tell myself.

Each day now is an adventurous one, and
out of Big Ben's chilling sight I can smilingly
claim all time my own. But not quite, I know,
all too aware of that other ticking clock, even if,
for the moment, I like to think it's stopped.

No Words of Love

Often the things not said are the most eloquent,
be it a flash of anger or the hurt in an eye, a hastily
wiped tear, the silence between moments of love,
a hug, a hand pressed in sympathy, a mother's
tender touch. How telling too the call not returned,
the letter still awaiting a reply, the cold stare from
across an unwelcoming room.

Words are too clumsy, too approximate, marshal
clichés far too readily. 'I love you' means so many
things... and nothing at all. So hush my darling,
no words of love tonight. You've hugged me tight
in wonder, anguish, joy and fear, as I have you.
There's little left for words to do.